THE MAKING OF
CHIPPING
NORTON

THE MAKING OF

CHIPPING NORTON

A GUIDE TO ITS BUILDINGS
AND HISTORY TO 1750

ADRIENNE ROSEN & JANICE CLIFFE

First published 2017

Phillimore, an imprint of The History Press
The Mill, Brimscombe Port
Stroud, Gloucestershire, GL5 2QG
www.thehistorypress.co.uk

British Library Cataloguing in Publication Data.
A catalogue record for this book is available from the British Library.

ISBN 978 0 7509 8116 3

Typesetting and origination by The History Press
Printed TJ Books Limited, Padstow, Cornwall

CONTENTS

ABOUT THE AUTHORS

ADRIENNE ROSEN is a historian with a special interest in towns. She was a lecturer in Local and Social History at Oxford University Department for Continuing Education, and is now an Emeritus Fellow of Kellogg College, Oxford.

JANICE CLIFFE spent fifty years as an architectural designer. She is a founding member of Chipping Norton Historical Research Group and Chipping Norton Buildings Record and has written several books on the buildings and history of Chipping Norton and Over Norton.

PREFACE AND ACKNOWLEDGEMENTS

C HIPPING NORTON today is an Oxfordshire market town of some 6,500 people, at the eastern edge of the Cotswolds. The handsome row of buildings along the upper side of its market place suggests a Georgian town, while the Town Hall and the impressive Bliss tweed mill in the valley testify to Chipping Norton's Victorian prosperity and its industrial past. But the town's history goes back much further than this, and by looking closely at its buildings and streets we can find survivals from earlier times all the way back to its medieval origins.

Most publications on Chipping Norton's history have concentrated on the centuries since 1750, after the enclosure of the town's open fields and the growth of its tweed industry, brewery and ironworks. Far less has been written about the town's early history for the good reason that clues to Chipping Norton's development are not easy to find. Very little archaeological investigation has been done in the town. The historian looking for documentary sources will find that few local records survive from the medieval period and the sixteenth and seventeenth centuries are only slightly better. The evidence of Chipping Norton's buildings is potentially a significant addition if we look at their location and relationship to the street, their materials, plans and style. We have chosen to focus on Chipping Norton before 1750, with the aim of bringing together what we can learn from the built environment with documentary evidence from printed sources and national and local archives. There is still much more to discover and understand and we hope that others will take our investigations further in the future.

This book is the result of a two-year project undertaken by a small voluntary group, the Chipping Norton Buildings Record, under the wing of the Oxfordshire Buildings Record. Our first thanks go to our fellow group members Paul Clark, Victoria Hubbard and John Marshall for their expertise and contributions, all combined to enable this publication to come to fruition. We are indebted to Historic England (formerly English Heritage) for funding both the project and this book as part of its 'Early Fabric in Historic Towns' scheme which aims to discover, record, understand and publicise early urban buildings and fabric, and we thank Rebecca Lane (Historic England) and David Clark (Oxfordshire Buildings Record) for their support and advice. Historic England also gave us access to the professional expertise of Dr Martin Bridge for tree-ring dating of oak timbers, and Dr Antonia Catchpole for analysis of the town's burgage plots.

The project would not have been possible without the interest and co-operation of the people of Chipping Norton. The owners and occupiers of houses, flats, pubs, shops, cafes, galleries and offices have welcomed us into their premises and allowed us to explore. Volunteers from the town and from further afield also took part in the initial surveys of the medieval streets. We are very grateful to them all.

Many others have helped us with our research, including the Chipping Norton Historical Research Group whose work on probate documents has been invaluable, and the archivists of the Oxfordshire History Centre, Gloucester and Worcester cathedrals, and Brasenose, Magdalen and Oriel colleges, Oxford. The trustees of Chipping Norton Museum gave us access to their archives and picture collection. Our thanks also go to James Bond, Jenny Harrington, Andrew Rosen and Trevor Rowley for their friendly advice and assistance.

The first part of this book, written by Adrienne Rosen, traces the development and changing fortunes of the town from its beginnings to about 1750, using new evidence from documents and buildings for an overview of Chipping Norton and its people in the past. The second part, written by Janice Cliffe, looks at each of the central streets in turn and takes the reader on a walk to explore both what remains and what was once there. We hope that people living in Chipping Norton today, visitors, local historians and buildings enthusiasts will enjoy discovering its history as much as we have done.

Adrienne Rosen and Janice Cliffe,
August 2017

ABBREVIATIONS

The following abbreviations are used:

Bodl.	Bodleian Library, Oxford
BNC	Brasenose College, Oxford
Cal. Pat.	*Calendar of Patent Rolls*
CNM	Chipping Norton Museum of Local History
d.	died
JOJ	*Jackson's Oxford Journal*
OHC	Oxfordshire History Centre, Oxford
OHS	Oxford Historical Society
ORS	Oxfordshire Record Society
TNA	The National Archives, Kew
VCH	*Victoria County History*
WODC	West Oxfordshire District Council

PART I

People, Town and Buildings of Chipping Norton to 1750

◄ 1 *Frontispiece:* Painting by an unknown artist of Chipping Norton market place, looking north, in the mid to late eighteenth century. The Talbot with its inn sign is at the right. In the centre is the old market house on the site of the present Town Hall. This view of the market place was reproduced a century later on the Oddfellows' banner shown on the front cover. (**By permission** of Chipping Norton Town Council)

CHAPTER ONE

THE MEDIEVAL TOWN, 1000–1540

C HIPPING NORTON is a medieval town, planned and laid out on a hillside. As far as we know the site was at that time uninhabited, but the landscape around it had already been shaped by settlers, farmers and travellers over many centuries. Flint and pottery finds in the area and monuments including the Rollright Stones nearby are evidence of prehistoric settlement and clearance, and in Roman times there was a villa or small settlement to the south-east near Glyme Farm, but the origins of Chipping Norton lie in an Anglo-Saxon village whose location is unknown.

ORIGINS: VILLAGE AND CASTLE

The earliest document to mention Chipping Norton is Domesday Book, which in 1086 listed the settlement of 'Norton' with fifty-three households, or between 200 and 300 people.[1] The name Norton means 'north settlement or estate' which suggests that it was established as a northern outpost of either Shipton-under-Wychwood, a royal manor, or Charlbury, which like Shipton had an important minster or mother-church. The need for a source of water, and the location of the church, both point to a location for the Anglo-Saxon settlement of Norton in the valley near the Common Brook. Traces of the early village must survive in the ground and no doubt they will be discovered one day by archaeologists.

Domesday Book also recorded the name of the new Norman lord of Chipping Norton, Ernulf de Hesdin from Picardy. Ernulf was given many manors in southern England by William the Conqueror, and he proved to

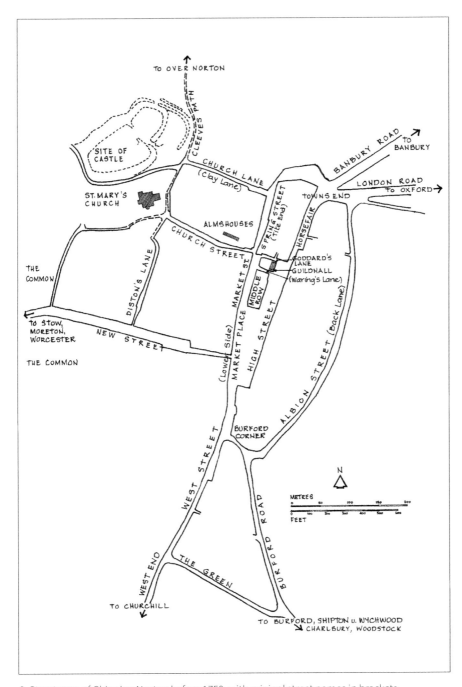

2 Street map of Chipping Norton before 1750, with original street names in brackets.

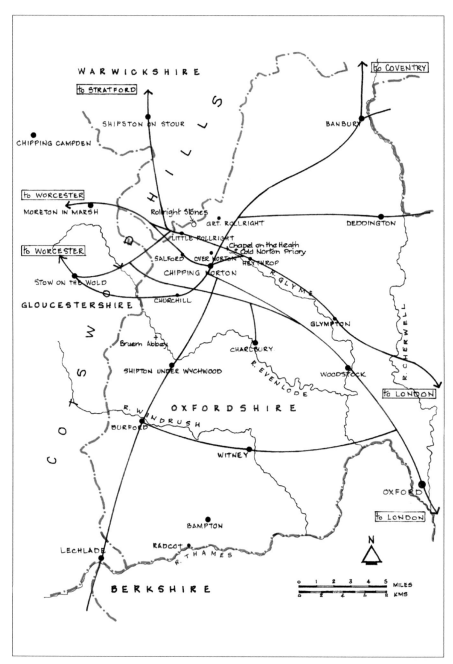

3 Medieval Chipping Norton in its locality, showing pre-1974 county boundaries, rivers and major routes.

be a skilful estate manager whose lands had increased in value by 1086. A document sealed in the 1090s by Ernulf in his house at Norton, in the presence of his wife and daughter, his sons, his chaplain and the knights of his household, tells us that he built a residence on his new estate, most likely a motte-and-bailey castle (a wooden tower set on an earthen mound or motte) on the earthwork now called the Castle Banks, or perhaps on the natural mound to the west now occupied by the Victorian house called The Mount. There was also a church at Norton. Ernulf and his wife Emmelina were generous benefactors to monasteries and they gave Norton's church to the Benedictine abbey at Gloucester.[2] This early church may have occupied the same site as the present parish church, but none of the original building has survived. The relationship between Chipping Norton's church and Gloucester has endured for more than 900 years, and the Dean and Chapter of Gloucester as successors to the abbey are still today the patrons who nominate each vicar.

The settlement was well connected with the wider world. From the north-west a major route from Worcester, Evesham and Stow-on-the-Wold passed just to the south of the modern town of Chipping Norton and on to Charlbury, Woodstock and Oxford. The name of Salford, a few miles to the west, indicates a route used for the transport of salt from Droitwich in Cheshire to south-east England. Another Anglo-Saxon route (the modern A361) ran from Banbury to Chipping Norton and then south to Shipton-under-Wychwood, Burford and the Thames crossing at Lechlade, and between these roads a network of trackways connected local communities.[3]

Ernulf's lands at Norton descended to his daughter Avelina and then to his grandson William Fitzalan, whose descendants were to be lords of Chipping Norton for many generations thereafter. Their principal estates were in Shropshire where the Fitzalans were powerful barons in the Welsh Marches. Chipping Norton was remote from their strongholds at Oswestry and Clun, but it was a profitable estate in prime sheep-farming country and conveniently situated on a route between the family's Shropshire lands and London. It was also within easy reach of the royal palace at Woodstock and the Forest of Wychwood where medieval kings enjoyed hunting with their nobles and counsellors. By 1300 the Fitzalans had transformed Norton with the construction of a stone castle, a church, a priory and a new town.

Impressive earthworks called the Castle Banks can be seen today to the north-west of the town, but very little is known about the castle that stood there and the site has never been excavated. The mound is divided

4 Aerial view of Chipping Norton in 1953 looking east with the church and the Castle Banks at lower left.

into two by a bank and ditch, and in both sections it is evident that the remains of stone buildings lie beneath the surface. Another bank to the east partially encloses a further small area, which could be the site of Ernulf de Hesdin's original motte and bailey. Below the steep north-west escarpment is the Brook where banks enclose a large medieval fishpond, now drained and known as Pool Meadow. The location of the castle's main gate is uncertain: was it on the north where there is a gap in the outer bank, on the east facing uphill to the town, or on the south looking towards the road from Shropshire?

Chipping Norton's castle appears to have been a fortified residence rather than a fortress. Due to its position on the side of a hill it had no moat, although there is a ditch on the south and west sides. It has been suggested that the castle was built in the early twelfth century or during the turbulent reign of Stephen, though it is not mentioned in written records, and the building probably underwent several phases of construction as the Fitzalans' plans for Chipping Norton changed. The formidable scale of the earthworks shows that someone amongst its medieval owners had plans for a grand residence, and the ambitious landscaping of the valley with its fishpond – similar to the medieval 'pleasaunce' or pleasure-ground laid out near the Fitzalans' castle at Clun – was probably associated with this phase, but it is not certain that plans for a substantial building were carried out. For much of its history the castle at Chipping Norton seems to have been occupied only intermittently. By the reign of Henry VI in the mid-fifteenth century a survey records that it was in poor condition and all that remained of its buildings were an 'ancient hall', a barn, a dovecote, a thatched cow-shed and a sheepcote, while the banks were used for grazing livestock.[4]

CREATING A NEW TOWN

Enterprising landowners across England and Europe created towns in the twelfth and thirteenth centuries as a way of maximising the income from their estates, as towns attracted trade and generated rents, tolls and fines. In Oxfordshire the towns of Burford and Banbury were well established by the mid 1100s. New research by Antonia Catchpole has concluded that Chipping Norton was probably founded in the mid to late 1100s, at the same period as the Bishop of Winchester's new town of Witney.[5]

If this date is correct, the lord responsible for creating Chipping Norton was William Fitzalan, who succeeded his father in 1160 and died in 1210. In Shropshire he inherited the lordship of Clun and laid out a new town adjoining its castle. At Chipping Norton, his grandmother Avelina had founded an Augustinian priory and hospital at Cold Norton between 1148 and 1158 on the site of the present Priory Farm, and gave the priory the family's manor of Over Norton. The grant was confirmed by William in 1204. The Fitzalans' act of piety would diminish their own income, but the foundation of a town, if successful, would far outweigh the loss.[6]

The basic requirements of a new town were a large central market area; house or burgage plots along the main streets; back lanes providing access to the backs of the plots, which could later be developed into streets if demand for housing increased; a church for the townspeople; roads to bring customers to the town; and in some cases a new residence for the lord. These elements were sufficiently flexible to be adapted to the geography of the chosen site and could incorporate existing roads or buildings, so no two town plans are exactly the same. In the case of Chipping Norton the founders saw no need to provide a lordly residence or a new parish church in the town as the castle and St Mary's stood nearby. The church was certainly rebuilt, and traces of a large twelfth-century arch in the east wall of the tower suggest that reconstruction coincided with the establishment of the new town. The size of the early church, close to its present length, reflects the intention to provide for a large community.

William Fitzalan's surveyors chose a site for the new town at some distance from the castle, the church and the early settlement of Norton. We can only guess at their intentions, but the site they selected on the hillside above the castle and the church offered ample space to lay out all the necessary facilities on a grand scale. The rocky slope was unsuited to cultivation so the new buildings would not occupy valuable arable land. Evidence of the area's earlier use for digging stone has been found in recent archaeological excavations on the plots behind the White Hart and nos 7-10 High Street which discovered quarry-pits of the eleventh or twelfth century.[7] Below ground, the geology of the hillside offered building stone and firm footings for substantial masonry. The upper side of the market place stands on bands of the local Chipping Norton Limestone and Clypeus Grit, while buildings on the lower side are on mudstone or clay. Most importantly, the site offered a reliable water supply as an alternative to the Brook, as the alternating strata of limestone, clay and marlstone result in springs which emerge from the hillside, notably along the line of Spring Street. The selection in the twelfth century of this site on the side of a hill, rising from 175m at the west end of New Street to over 210m above Albion Street, has had practical consequences throughout Chipping Norton's history and the steep slope is still one of the town's defining characteristics.

The line of High Street and the market place probably followed an existing track. Medieval routes tended to be corridors consisting of several parallel tracks, especially when crossing difficult terrain such as a hillside, so that the traveller could choose the path with the surest footing. Modern Albion Street appears to have been the main trackway on the Banbury-Shipton route, continuing as the main route south from Chipping Norton along the Burford road. A line of field boundaries suggests another parallel track further up the hill east of Albion Street, meeting the Burford road at the junction with The Green, while lower down was another parallel path, which continued southwards to the village of Churchill. From these alternatives the medieval surveyors chose the lowest as the high street of the new town, with Albion Street as the back lane providing rear access to burgage plots. Long-distance routes now entered the town at the north-east from Banbury, Stratford and Oxford, and at the south-east from Woodstock and Charlbury.

The road from Worcester and Stow from the west (now the A44) did not originally pass through Chipping Norton, however, but crossed the Common (where a hollow way still shows the medieval route) to join the Burford road south of the town on the way to London. In order to bring travellers into the market place, the road was diverted further north and became known as New Street. We cannot tell whether New Street was created when the town was established, or in the fourteenth or fifteenth century, and its name only appears in documents from 1545.[8]

The heart of a medieval town was its space for markets and fairs. Chipping Norton's cigar-shaped market place as originally laid out was one of the largest in Oxfordshire, extending nearly 500m from north to south and 75m from east to west, even broader than it is today because the building frontage on the upper side has gradually moved forward. Entrances to the market place were narrow in order to control access. Further down the hill New Street widens out considerably, and this area was used as a suburban market place for cattle in the seventeenth century. West Street too has several points at which the roadway widens into possible suburban market areas.

William Fitzalan's surveyors laid out house plots along both the upper and lower sides of the market place. The aim was to attract settlers who would construct their own buildings, so the plots were offered as 'burgages', free from the manorial services required from the lord's tenants in the countryside and subject only to a small annual rent. Analysis of medieval town plans has shown that burgages in planned towns were generally laid out according to standard measurements based on a statute perch (a length of 16½ft or 5.03m). Measurement of the building frontages along the upper side of Chipping Norton's market place shows that the original plots were 1½ perches, and no. 19 High Street still occupies an original plot of that width. The length of the plots varies with the curve of Albion Street as their eastern boundary, and one of the longest plots in the centre of High Street, White Hart Mews, extends to 120m. These long narrow plots are

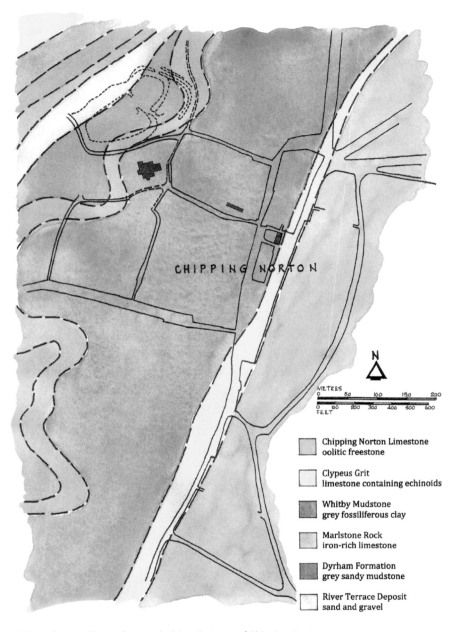

N

METRES
0   50   100   150   200

0   100   200   300   400   500   600
FEET

	Chipping Norton Limestone oolitic freestone
	Clypeus Grit limestone containing echinoids
	Whitby Mudstone grey fossiliferous clay
	Marlstone Rock iron-rich limestone
	Dyrham Formation grey sandy mudstone
	River Terrace Deposit sand and gravel

5 Map showing the geology underlying the town of Chipping Norton.

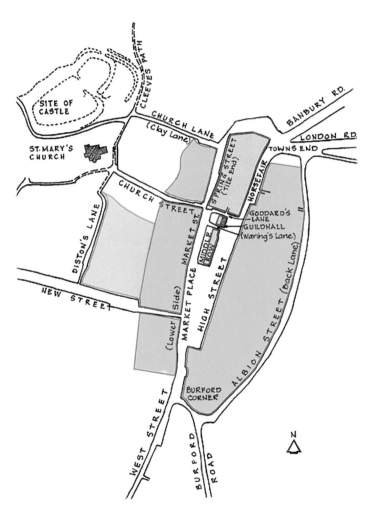

6 Map showing areas laid out with burgage plots (red) and possible plots in New Street (green). Later medieval infill in the market place is shown in blue.

7 Aerial view of the market place from the north in 1929. Albion Street (left) was the back lane for the long thin burgage plots along High Street on the east side of the market place. The pattern is less clear on the west side where the plots are broader and shorter.

typical of medieval burgages in prime commercial areas where the aim was to maximise the number of plots with a frontage to the market place. Wealthy purchasers could combine adjoining plots to construct impressive houses, such as no. 23 High Street (the Crown & Cushion) which stands on a 2½-perch plot with a frontage of 13.27m created from one original burgage plus most of the neighbouring plot.

While the burgage plots on the upper side of the market place stretched up the hill, those on the lower side were laid out on an equally steep downhill slope and most of them had no back lane. In order to make plots on the lower side equally attractive with an area similar to those on High Street, the lower side burgage plots were wider at 2 perches (about 10m) and about 17 perches (87m) long. No. 15 Market Place, for instance, occupies a 2-perch plot with a frontage of 10.13m. Areas of ridge and furrow – medieval strips formed by ploughing, preserved as undulating grassland when the fields were later enclosed for pasture – can still be seen north-west of the town on the eastern side of the Brook, and the open fields of the original settlement may well have extended further south, with Church Lane, Church Street and Diston's Lane originating as slightly raised field-paths between blocks of strips. The western boundary of the house-plots on the west side of Spring Street between Church Street and Church Lane has a slight reverse S-shaped curve which may reflect an original field boundary or field strip.

Another block of burgages stood on the west side of West Street as far as no. 11, while on the east side of West Street the plots form part of the High Street series of burgages bounded by Albion Street, extending as far south as the King's Arms at Burford Corner. It is not clear whether the plots along the north side of New Street were part of the original town plan; they ran back to the line of a watercourse and appear to be of similar length to those above the market place, although later development has obscured the plot boundaries. On the south side of New Street the picture is even less clear, and if plots were laid out here when the town was founded they were either not taken up or were abandoned later.

A new town was a speculative venture and not all medieval foundations were successful, but Chipping Norton attracted settlers and traders from the outset and in 1204 King John granted William Fitzalan an annual three-day fair in the town. The weekly market was probably already well established without a royal grant. The success of the new town also resulted in an addition to its name, when the prefix 'chipping', meaning market, was added to Norton. A document from 1218 is the earliest found so far to use the new name, and by 1300 the town was known as 'Chepyngnorton'.[9]

DEVELOPMENT OF THE TOWN PLAN

Once a medieval town was laid out, its buildings and street-plan could be adapted by the inhabitants to suit their own needs. Chipping Norton appears to have been planned by the Fitzalans as a large settlement, intended perhaps as a major Cotswold wool-marketing centre, but before long it must have become clear that the blueprint had been too ambitious. Perhaps it proved difficult to attract tenants for all the plots available. The solution was to shorten the market place to about half its original length. At the southern end, the original entrance may have been by the King's Arms at Burford Corner; if so, a new narrow entrance further north was created in the twelfth or thirteenth century by extending the building line on the east side of West Street further into the roadway. The extension created a right-angled south-east corner to the market place which is mentioned in a document of 1302, so this must have been an early change to the original town plan.

At the northern end of the market place, the area beyond Goddard's Lane is now occupied by the buildings between Horsefair and Spring Street and is no longer part of the market space. Encroachment on this large area began early in the town's history. New evidence from dendrochronology tells us that the Chequers premises on the north side of Goddard's Lane were constructed in the mid fifteenth century, so the area must have been available for building by that date. Reports of a richly moulded stone arch which once stood in Guildhall Yard on the north side of the lane, possibly a thirteenth- or fourteenth-century doorway, suggest that building had started here much earlier.[10] Once the castle was no longer in use the northern end of the town would have been a less prestigious area. The narrow northern entrance to the market place from Horsefair dates back to the sixteenth century if not earlier. The burgage plots at the north end of High Street would always have been less attractive, being shorter and more distant from the commercial heart of the town, and there is evidence of farm buildings here in the seventeenth century.

MEDIEVAL PEOPLE

From the thirteenth century onwards, legal and administrative documents begin to provide glimpses of individual people at Chipping Norton. Alice de Witney petitioned the king for justice after being beaten and imprisoned for complaining about the size of a loaf of bread bought from the wife of William Trotyn, bailiff of Chipping Norton. Richard Wine gave his land in 'Stockewellestrete' (perhaps West Street or Burford Road) to Cold Norton Priory. A list of taxpayers in 1316 named sixty-six townsmen and two women. Two of the three most highly assessed were the lord of the manor and his bailiff, but the wealthiest man in Chipping Norton was William Smyt (the smith). They were followed on the list by a group of merchants including William and Nicholas Aleyn, Laurence Pope and Adam Breton. Occupational surnames suggest trades and crafts in the town, such as Richard le Irmonger, John le Tanner and Thomas le Spicer, and surnames derived from place-names show people moving into Chipping Norton from the surrounding area, such as Robert de Cornwelle and Richard de Teynton.[11]

One of the taxpayers in 1316 was Robert in Angulo or Robert 'in the corner'. His name also appeared on a writ of 1302, this time in medieval English as Robert de la Hurne, from herne or hurne meaning a corner or nook. His name tells us where he lived, at no. 1 Market Place east of the Fox Hotel, where there used to be a sharply angled south-east corner to the market place (demolished in 1893 when Cattle Market was cut through, replacing one of the burgage plots), and a later document describes this house as 'the messuage heretofore called Harneplace' or the house in the corner. Robert de la Hurne must have been a leading townsman in 1302 as he was one of two chosen to represent Chipping Norton in Parliament, a privilege that the town relinquished soon afterwards.[12]

The early fourteenth century was a time of economic depression in England, followed in 1348-49 and again in 1361 by the devastating outbreaks of plague known as the Black Death. In many towns including Witney there is evidence of vacant houses and shops and the abandonment of outlying areas of settlement but no records have survived from Chipping Norton to document the impact of the plague. The countryside of north-west Oxfordshire was badly affected, and the canons of Cold Norton Priory nearby complained that a shortage of labourers left them unable to cultivate their land. The parish priests of Chipping Norton, Little Rollright,

8 The south-east corner of the market place before 1893.

Chastleton, Enstone and Charlbury all died in 1349-50. A poll tax levied in 1377 on men and women over the age of 14 was paid by 304 people at Chipping Norton, amounting to a total population of approximately 500, fewer than Burford and significantly smaller than Witney or Banbury.[13]

The Fitzalan family, now earls of Arundel with estates in Sussex as well as Shropshire, had held the manor of Chipping Norton for more than 200 years. Richard, third earl of Arundel, was one of the richest men in four-teenth-century England. His lands in the Welsh Marches and Sussex were managed as a single estate, specialising in sheep, horse and cattle-rearing with sales of wool from the earl's flocks of thousands of sheep. It was the third earl who transferred the family's main residence from Shropshire to Arundel, and on his death in 1376 he was the first Fitzalan to be buried in Sussex. Not long before he died the earl gave three of his manors in Sussex to his granddaughter Philippa when she married Sir Richard Sergeaux, a Cornish knight. Her husband, however, wanted an Oxfordshire estate, and in about 1380 he persuaded Richard, the fourth earl, to exchange the three Sussex manors for Chipping Norton. Thus the manor was separated from the Arundel lands, and after Philippa's death in 1399 it descended in the families of her three daughters.[14]

WOOL TOWN AND MARKET TOWN

Medieval Chipping Norton has been aptly described as a 'wool town'. Its location at the edge of the Cotswolds, an area which produced high-quality wool much in demand in both Northern and Southern Europe, brought wealth to the merchants or 'woolmen' in the town who acted as middle-men between wool-growers and their wholesale customers. The trade was well established by the thirteenth century, and in 1279 Juliana le Breton of Chipping Norton, widow of the merchant Adam Breton, contracted to sell five sacks of wool to the Riccardi firm of Lucca in Italy with delivery to the port of Boston in Lincolnshire for shipping. Each sack of wool contained the clip of 260 sheep and weighed 364lbs, so five sacks would require a strong cart to transport the wool from Oxfordshire to the east coast. Richard le Faytour of Chipping Norton supplied wool to the Frescobaldi merchants of Florence in 1311, and Robert Bruton sent wool to London in 1339 for export to Antwerp and in 1348 petitioned the king for payment of a debt for 'good Cotswold wool'.[15]

The names of several of Chipping Norton's fifteenth-century woolmen appear on their memorial brasses in the parish church. John Yonge, 'sometyme wolman of this towne' who died in 1451, is portrayed with his feet resting on bales of wool. His son-in-law Thomas Gerveys was one of many local woolmen in 1475 shipping Cotswold wool through an Italian merchant at Southampton. Chipping Norton was the home of some leading merchants, although much of their work was done outside the town, settling contracts and making payments to sheep-farmers, negotiating sales with London merchants and arranging for the storage, packing and transport of wool. No specialised premises were needed, and sacks of wool were probably stored in outbuildings later described as barns behind Chipping Norton's High Street tenements with access for carts from the back lane.[16]

While the wool trade generated healthy profits for the woolmen, it could not provide employment for the whole town and by the fifteenth century there is evidence of many other occupations at Chipping Norton. Brasses in the church portrayed mercers such as John Stokes who sold fine imported and English-made fabrics, spices and a wide range of imported goods. John Pargeter, a Chipping Norton ironmonger, bought a shop in Woodstock in 1461. Ironmongery seems to have been a speciality of the town, and Thomas Smith of Chipping Norton supplied ironware including buckets, nails and iron window fixtures for the belltower of Merton College chapel at Oxford, which was built between 1448 and 1451. The town also had leather-workers such as tanners and shoemakers, suppliers of food and drink such as grocers, bakers, butchers and innkeepers, and other occupations including a draper, a chapman, a weaver and a chandler making candles. Chipping Norton's prosperity in the fifteenth century was based on both its role in the wool trade and its success as a market town.[17]

9 Brass of John and Isabel Yonge.

THE PARISH CHURCH AND CHANTRIES

The most distinguished building in Chipping Norton is the parish church of St Mary the Virgin, and its later medieval development was closely connected to the wealth of the town's leading citizens. The early fourteenth century saw the construction of both a new outer north aisle and a new or rebuilt south aisle. The south aisle is of particularly high quality, built in ashlar stone with its east wall filled by a huge six-light window with Decorated tracery. Outside, the south entrance has a rare hexagonal two-storied porch; only two other hexagonal church porches are known, at Bristol and Ludlow, and Chipping Norton's fourteenth-century wool merchants would certainly have been familiar with Ludlow's parish church of St Laurence. Nothing is known of the donors but the considerable cost of the south aisle and porch was probably the gift of Chipping Norton's own wealthy parishioners.

An even more ambitious project was undertaken in the mid fifteenth century when the nave was completely rebuilt. The design of the pillars, similar to those in the nave of Canterbury Cathedral, suggests that the mason John Smyth who worked at Canterbury and later designed Eton College chapel was involved at Chipping Norton. Below the heightened roof is an almost continuous range of clerestory windows which fill the church with light, while a great window with both interior and exterior stone tracery faces east above the chancel arch, the only Oxfordshire example of a feature found in several Gloucestershire churches funded by the profits of the wool trade. The prior of Worcester made a small donation to the fabric of the church in 1447-48 and contributions were probably received from other local landowners, but again it is likely that construction was funded largely from within the town. The wealthy woolman or ironmonger who supported the adornment of his parish church hoped for both spiritual and social benefits from his gift. Work continued on the church in the early sixteenth century when Richard Smyth left a bequest in 1502 'to the building of our Lady Chapel'.[18]

Within the church, parishioners established chantries to employ a priest who would celebrate daily Masses and pray for the souls of the benefactor and his or her family. A chantry dedicated to St Mary had been founded a century earlier. Two more were established in the newly rebuilt church, one in 1481 at the altar of St John the Baptist by Margaret Gerveys, the widow and daughter of woolmen, and another in 1497 at the altar of St James

10 Chipping Norton church from the north-east. The tower was rebuilt in 1825.

11 The early fourteenth-century south aisle and its Decorated window. The original steeply pitched roof was replaced by a shallower roof when the clerestory was built in the fifteenth century.

12 Clerestory windows.

13 East clerestory window above the chancel arch.

14 The heightened nave, looking west.

for Margaret Pynner from another wool-dealing family, her two husbands and her parents. The foundation of a chantry was an expensive business as it required sufficient land and property to be given as an endowment to support the priest and maintain the altar in perpetuity. Many houses and cottages in the town came to be owned by one of the chantries and the rental income was paid to the priest.[19]

Until 1502 none of Chipping Norton's manorial lords had been buried in the church – indeed, some had probably never even visited the town. A resident lord was a new experience for the town when Richard Croft settled there after acquiring one-third of the manor in 1481. Croft was a younger son from a powerful family in the Welsh Marches who entered royal service with Edward IV as keeper of the royal palace at Woodstock and controller of the king's building works there. He lost his posts at Woodstock when Henry VII defeated the Yorkists in 1485 and this may have prompted his move to Chipping Norton, where he remained active in local administration as an Oxfordshire JP.[20]

Croft must have worshipped in the church and watched its development in the late fifteenth century; perhaps he also lent his expertise and connections from his experience with the royal building works at Woodstock. In his will he asked to be buried in Chipping Norton church in the chapel of St John the Baptist, and after his death in 1502 – or more likely after the death of his widow Anne in 1509 – a richly carved tomb-chest was commissioned, bearing alabaster effigies of the couple. Richard is portrayed in armour as befitted a gentleman, his feet resting on a lion. Traces of colour including red colouring and a fine gold border on Anne's gown show that both figures were originally brightly painted. From its style it is likely that the tomb was carved at one of the leading alabaster workshops in Derbyshire or Staffordshire.[21]

A second rich tomb (which has not survived) was placed in the newly completed Lady Chapel at about the same date for John Ashfield, lord of the manor of Heythrop, who died in 1506. The Ashfields lived only three miles from Chipping Norton and were closely involved with the town. Like the Crofts and the Fitzalans, the family came originally from the Welsh Marches. It has been suggested that this John Ashfield (d. 1506) or his father John (d. 1455) were wool-merchants who paid for the building of the nave at Chipping Norton, but this is unlikely. Both were gentlemen, not merchants, even if some of their income derived from sheep-farming. The older John Ashfield in 1455 requested burial not at Chipping Norton but in 'the

15 Tomb of Richard and Anne Croft, *c.*1509.

16 Finely carved angels on the Croft tomb. Their faces were later destroyed, possibly at the Reformation.

chapel of St Mary the Virgin of Cold Norton', probably Chapel on the Heath where construction in the eighteenth century uncovered stone coffins containing bones, beads and a silver crucifix. The younger John Ashfield was still a child in the 1450s when work on the nave was under way. Both father and son may well have contributed to the cost of rebuilding the nave and chapels of Chipping Norton church, and their coat of arms with three mullets (stars) are among others still to be seen there, but the Ashfields were by no means the only patrons.[22]

THE GUILD OF THE HOLY TRINITY

In October 1450, while work on the new nave was still under way, the vicar and four leading townsmen paid £40 for a royal licence to found a guild associated with the church, to be known as the guild of the Holy Trinity. The guild was to maintain two chaplains to celebrate Mass daily, and would support 'a fit person freely to instruct in the rudiments of grammar the poor boys and scholars coming to Chepyngnorton'. It was to be a permanent body, governed by an annually elected master and authorised to acquire property to fund its activities.[23]

Guilds or fraternities of this kind were popular in the fifteenth century and could be found in every important town. Their role was partly religious, and the Trinity guild had its own chapel in Chipping Norton church; on the north side of the chancel arch three niches can be seen behind the pulpit, remnants of a chapel enclosed by wooden screens that were destroyed at the Reformation. Guild members met for Mass on Trinity Sunday before holding their annual feast and electing new officers, and candles and torches were provided for members' funerals. Charitable activities were also important, and in 1535 the guild maintained an almshouse for six paupers as well as the grammar school in Church Street, providing facilities for the town that were administered by townsmen rather than the lord of the manor.

Equally important was the guild's role as a social club for the upper and middle ranks of town society, both male and female. Members of neighbouring gentry families such as the Ashfields also joined Chipping Norton's guild. Like the chantries, the guild received gifts and bequests and gradually built up a large collection of local property that could be leased to members at attractive rates. In 1535 the guild's annual income, mostly from rents, was £11 5s. Business dealings were promoted by social contacts between the

17 Niches which once formed the east wall of the Trinity guild chapel, its other sides consisting of wooden screens. A fifteenth-century interior chapel in a similar position can be seen in Burford's parish church.

18 The Guildhall. The building has been extended since the sixteenth century to the left of the central doorway, and to the right of the first-floor windows.

town's merchants and members from a wider area. The survival of guild records elsewhere shows that Chipping Norton men and their wives joined the guild at Stratford-upon-Avon in the fifteenth and sixteenth centuries, and merchants from Chipping Norton were also members of the popular town guild at Ludlow; if Chipping Norton's guild membership records had survived they would no doubt include names from these towns and others on major trade routes.[24]

A guild needed a hall in which to conduct its business and gather for feasting and sociability, and this was the purpose of the Guildhall, which can be seen today in Middle Row. Timber used in the roof and in ground-floor ceiling beams and a lintel was felled between 1514 and 1520, showing that the building dates from the early sixteenth century and may have replaced earlier guild premises. The Guildhall as originally constructed had at least three bays. Four pairs of early Tudor windows can be seen on the first floor in the oldest section, three on the east and one on the west, lighting the Holy Trinity guild's meeting hall which was a large first-floor room open to the roof. On the ground floor is a fine Tudor doorway facing east towards High Street.

CHIPPING NORTON IN THE EARLY 1500S

What would a visitor to the town in the reign of Henry VIII have seen? Unfortunately none of the travellers who passed through Chipping Norton has left us their impressions, but by bringing together the evidence of surviving buildings with written records we can build up a picture of the early Tudor town. More details and illustrations of individual buildings can be found in the later chapters on each of the medieval streets.

By 1500 Chipping Norton was already a town built of stone. The local grey limestone was readily available from small quarries around the parish, including some very close to the town. In 1471 a tenement in the 'upper street' (High Street) was conveyed with half an acre 'at the end extending to the quarry', evidently a burgage plot stretching up the hill to a quarry beyond the back lane. Thomas Fryday, a mason in the town who made his will in 1545, was in demand over a wide area and was owed money for work at Bruern Abbey (dissolved nine years earlier), a window at Hanwell Castle and battlements on the church at King's Sutton near Banbury.[25] Cottages and outbuildings were probably thatched but the traditional roof covering for more substantial buildings was locally produced limestone slates. Timber was used for roofs, and sometimes for timber-framing above ground-floor level, as well as interior features such as staircases, doors and floors. Both oak and elm were available locally and are found in Chipping Norton's historic buildings, with elm gradually replacing the more costly oak from the sixteenth century onwards. Where oak in buildings does survive it can sometimes be dated by dendrochronology based on the number and spacing of tree-rings, telling us when the tree was felled and the likely date of construction.

The plan laid out for the town by William Fitzalan in the twelfth century had been modified but it was still centred on the spacious market place with the houses of the social and economic elite along its upper and lower sides. Even here there was sufficient space for houses to be built parallel to the street rather than sideways along a narrow burgage plot. In 1500 these houses were probably more varied in style than today, with lower rooflines. The market place was the centre of public life and the location of the high cross. Another essential facility was a gaol, and in the early seventeenth century a tenement near the south end of Middle Row called the Stock House was rebuilt with a prison beneath, presumably with a set of stocks in it, and a shop and chamber above.[26] Beneath no. 20 High Street is a notable medieval

19 A typical rubble wall of local limestone at Chipping Norton. Roughly similar-sized stones are arranged in horizontal lines or courses.

20 Cotswold stone slates, laid with smaller slates at the top near the ridge and larger ones lower down near the eaves. The slates hang from pins attached to wooden battens.

survival, a vaulted undercroft which has been dated to the late fourteenth century. The undercroft's fine medieval workmanship led the Victorians to believe that this was a chapel or a monastery, but in fact it was more likely a tavern accessible down steps from the street, similar to medieval undercrofts found in Burford, Oxford and other medieval towns.[27]

The sixteenth-century visitor to the town had a choice of at least two inns. In 1428 Robert Stratford owned the Crown, also known as the Crown upon the Hoop, and the George is mentioned in 1549. Perhaps one of these was the inn later called the White Hart, for inns and pubs frequently changed their names. Situated at the centre of High Street (no. 16) in one of the most prestigious and visible locations in the town, the White Hart (now White Hart Mews) may be a purpose-built late medieval inn, and the addition of a timber-framed jettied gallery at the rear in the fifteenth or early sixteenth century to provide more accommodation tells us that it was profitable.[28]

The western side of the market place, now Market Place and Market Street, was known as the Nether Row or Lower Side. Houses were probably constructed here when the town was first built, at the same time as those in High Street. Buildings on the lower side have been less thoroughly modernised over the centuries, however, so there are more early features surviving here. A substantial medieval house discovered behind the seventeenth-century frontages of nos 8 and 9 Market Street had a hall open to the roof, and using dendrochronology the oak timbers have been dated to between 1424 and 1456. It was clearly a fine residence, and shows that not all of Chipping Norton's prestigious medieval houses were in High Street. From the front windows of houses in Market Street the full width of the market place could be seen until buildings began to appear in Middle Row. Evidence from some of the surviving buildings as well as documents suggests that Middle Row started to encroach on the market place from the middle of the fifteenth century.[29] The row probably developed gradually as the town's economy prospered and the demand for premises increased.

Our survey of the late medieval town becomes much more speculative when we leave the market place to explore the side-streets. The area around the junction of the Banbury and London roads was known as Cocks Towns End, a name which dates back to the fourteenth century or earlier although its meaning is a mystery. Medieval towns took care to mark the boundaries of their jurisdiction, and Cocks Towns End was literally the end of the town. Spring Street was known as Tite End from the regional word 'tite' meaning a spring or public water supply. This was a wet area, less healthy than the higher ground. Other street names also reflected the damp conditions, including Clay Lane, the old name for Church Lane, and its continuation Watery Lane between the Castle Banks and the churchyard. The management of water flowing down the hillside has always been a feature of Chipping Norton, and stone culverts can be found in cellars and in many locations in the lower half of the town.

Church Lane leads directly to the Castle Banks, and we might assume that this had been the main approach to the castle gate – yet instead of a busy street lined with houses we find today a narrow country lane between a field to the north and a large Victorian house and its gardens to the south. As the castle was built before the town was laid out it is unlikely that its gate-house would have been placed here, facing up the hill and thus difficult to defend, and a main entrance on the south or south-west is more likely. Once Chipping Norton was established, however, it would be convenient to have a side gate here leading directly along Church Lane into the market place. The decline of the castle was probably a factor in the decision to abandon the northern section of the early market place, and as a result the town's social and commercial centre moved further south. A document mentions a tenement in 'Clay Street' (Church Lane) in about 1330, but in 1453 Cold Norton Priory held a croft or enclosed piece of pasture in Church Lane between two other crofts, either land never built upon or the site of decayed houses, possibly abandoned after the Black Death.[30] From the early sixteenth century the vacant land and abundant water supply in Church Lane were put to use in a tannery. Tanning produced very unpleasant smells and the industry was usually located away from residential areas – another clue that this north-west corner of Chipping Norton was neither densely populated nor prestigious by 1500.

Church Street, the direct route between the parish church and the market place, was the site in 1500 of several buildings associated with the church. At the lower end stood the grammar school, maintained by the guild of the Holy Trinity, with accommodation for the schoolmaster. Also in this street were two of the three large chantry houses, occupied by the chantry priests of St James and St John. Another mansion belonging to the chantry of St Mary was in 'le church lane', probably Diston's Lane. These houses were part of the chantries' endowment and they may have been the former homes of the wealthy parishioners for whose souls the chantry priests offered their prayers.[31]

New Street was the main route into Chipping Norton from Stow and the north-west, with a narrow entrance into the market place at the top of the hill (widened in 1969 when a row of houses was demolished to accommodate modern traffic). In 1500 the most impressive sight in New Street would have been the new manor house halfway up, on the site now occupied by the former British School. This was the home of Richard Croft, the first lord of the manor to live in the town for many years, constructed in the last twenty years of the fifteenth century. A later lease described it as 'built with stone' – possibly re-used masonry from the castle ruins – with courtyards, outhouses, barns and stables, gardens and orchards. From here Croft supervised the farming of his estate, including the production of wool, which he sold directly to merchants in London, and conducted business as lord of the manor and a county JP.[32]

West Street was the site of another large late fifteenth-century house, built by Gloucester Abbey as the rectors of the parish. Originally known as the 'parsonage house', this was the farmhouse for the abbey's holding of four yardlands (80 acres) and for the collection of all the tithes on crops and livestock produced in Chipping Norton and Over Norton. The house still stands and is now called the Manor House. A lease from the abbey in 1504 required the tenant to build a chimney and to keep in good repair all the buildings, including a dovecote, as well as maintaining the chancel of the church and paying the vicar's stipend of £8 a year.[33]

CONCLUSION

Chipping Norton's largest medieval buildings are well known. The parish church, the Guildhall, the jettied range behind the White Hart and the fourteenth-century undercroft below no. 20 High Street have long been recognised as features of a prosperous wool town with wealth to invest in building. From the recent survey of the town we have learned that these are not the only medieval survivals, however, for parts of medieval houses survive in cellars and behind later frontages, and medieval timbers were re-used in later construction. The survivals can be found all around the medieval market place, particularly along the lower side in Market Street and Spring Street, an area that fell out of fashion in later centuries and did not undergo wholesale rebuilding. The survey has also shown that at Chipping Norton stone was the predominant building material from an early date; if there was a method of dating stone, we would certainly discover much more re-used medieval material.

The names of a few of the town's most prominent medieval citizens have come down to us but otherwise we know little about its people and their lives. In the period from 1540 to 1660, from the Reformation until the Restoration following the Civil War, the documentary sources become both more abundant and more revealing. For the first time we can see individual people and their homes and workplaces so that Chipping Norton's society and economy begin to come into sharper focus, as the next chapter will show.

Notes to Chapter 1

1   http://opendomesday.org

2   E. Miller (ed.), *Agrarian History of England and Wales*, ii *(1042-1350)*, 118-19; J.H. Round, *Calendar of Documents preserved in France 918-1206*, 481-2; C. Johnson and H.A. Cronne (eds), *Regesta Regum Anglo-Normannorum 1066-1154*, ii (1956), 296, 410.

3   *VCH Oxon.* x. 127; F.T.S. Houghton, 'Salt-ways', *Birmingham & Warws. Archaeological Society*, 54 (1929-30), 10, 15; D. Hooke, *The Anglo-Saxon Landscape: The Kingdom of the Hwicce* (2009), 215.

4   TNA, SC11/33.

5   A. Catchpole, 'An analysis of the plan and development of Chipping Norton, Oxon' (unpublished report 2015). This account of the town's development is based substantially on Antonia Catchpole's work.

6   *VCH Oxon.* ii. 95-6.

7   E. Simons, J. Phimester, L. Webley and A. Smith, 'A late medieval inn at the White Hart Hotel, Chipping Norton, Oxfordshire', *Oxoniensia*, 70 (2005), 309-23; P. Lovett, 'An archaeological watching brief at Albion Street, Chipping Norton' (Worcester Archaeology, unpublished report 2015), 1-20.

8   OHC, MS Wills Oxon 179.90 (will of William Hunt 1545).

9   Gazetteer of Markets and Fairs in England and Wales to 1516: www.history.ac.uk/cmh/gaz/gazweb2.html; *Pipe Roll 2 Henry III* (Pipe Roll Society n.s. 39), 84.

10 J.H. Parker, *The Ecclesiastical and Architectural Topography of England* (1850); C. Kirtland, *Memorials of Chipping Norton* (1871), 19, 76.

11 TNA, SC8/79/3904; BNC, Hurst Catalogue vol.5, f.1; TNA, E179/161/8.

12 F. Palgrave (ed.), *Parliamentary Writs*, i, 677; Chipping Norton Town Clerk's Office, documents, Wm. Heathcott to Henry Cornish 1604.

13 *VCH Oxon.* xiv. 75; *Calendar of Papal Letters, v, 1396-1404*, 198; A.H. Thompson, 'Registers of John Gynewell, Bishop of Lincoln, for the years 1347-50', *Archaeological Journal*, 68 (1911), 355; C.C. Fenwick (ed.), *The Poll Taxes of 1377, 1379 and 1381* (pt 2, 2001), 291.

14 C. Given-Wilson, 'Wealth and credit, public and private: the earls of Arundel 1306-1397', *English Historical Review*, 106 (1991), 1-26; Miller, *Agrarian History 1042-1350*, 484-90; M. Clough (ed.), *Two Estate Surveys of the Fitzalan Earls of Arundel* (Sussex Record Society 67, 1969), pp.xxv-xxvi, 89-90, 176; www.historyofparliamentonline.org (see under Cergeaux).

15 A.R. Bell, C. Brooks and P.R. Dryburgh, *The English Wool Market c.1230-1327* (2007), 163, 182; *Calendar of Fine Rolls 1337-47*, 109; TNA, SC 8/13/616.

16 A.A. Ruddock, *Italian Merchants and Shipping in Southampton, 1270-1600* (Southampton Record Series 1951), 90.

17 F.N. Davis (ed.), *Parochial Collections of Wood and Rawlinson, i* (ORS 2, 1920), 90-2; *VCH Oxon.* xii. 361; J.E. Thorold Rogers (ed.), *Oxford City Documents, Financial and Judicial 1268-1665* (OHS 18, 1891), 314-37.

18 J.H. Harvey, *The Perpendicular Style* (1978), 186; Worcester Cathedral Library, C398 (prior's accounts 1447-8); TNA, PROB 11/13 (will of Richard Smyth 1503).

19 *VCH Oxon.* ii. 16; *Cal. Pat. 1476-85*, 277; *Cal. Pat. 1494-1509*, 109; A. Hanham, *The Celys and their World* (1985), 151.

20 C.S.L. Davies, 'The Crofts: creation and defence of a family enterprise under the Yorkists and Henry VII', *Historical Research*, 68 (1995), 241-65; *Cal. Pat. 1476-85*, 247-8.

21 TNA, PROB 11/13 (will of Richard Croft 1502); unpublished conservation report on Croft tomb by S. and L. Kelland (2015); R. Knowles and P. Routh, *The Medieval Monuments of Harewood* (1983), 46-51.

22 TNA, PROB 11/4 (will of John Ashfield 1455); PROB 11/15 (will of John Ashfield 1506); T. Phillipps (ed.), *Oxfordshire Monumental Inscriptions from the*

MSS of Anthony Wood, Dr Hutton and Mr Hinton (Evesham, 1825), 77; J.H. Parker, in *Proceedings of Oxford Architectural and Historical Society* n.s. 3 (1872-80), 280-1; W. Camden, *Britannia*, ed. R. Gough (1789), i. 295.

23 *Cal. Pat. 1446-52*, 402.

24 *Valor Ecclesiasticus*, ii (1814), 180-1; M. Macdonald (ed.), *The Register of the Guild of Stratford-upon-Avon* (Dugdale Society 2007); R.A. Griffiths, 'After Glyn Dwr: an age of reconciliation?', *Proceedings of British Academy*, 117 (2001 Lectures), 151.

25 *Calendar of Ancient Deeds*, v, p.126; OHC, MS Wills Oxon 179.147 (will of Thomas Fryday 1546).

26 OHC, MS Wills Oxon 178.46 (will of Richard Tanty 1531); TNA, STAC 8/162/7.

27 A. Catchpole, D. Clark and R. Peberdy, *Burford: Buildings and People in a Cotswold Town* (2008), 70-1.

28 TNA, C1/7/68; *Calendar of Close Rolls 1422-9*, 453; *Cal. Pat. 1548-9*, 194; Simons, 'A late medieval inn', 316-18.

29 W.H. Turner and H.O. Coxe, *Calendar of Charters and Rolls in the Bodleian Library* (1878), 278.

30 BNC, Hurst Catalogue vol.5, ff.8, 30.

31 *Cal. Pat. 1548-9*, 192, 414-15.

32 Chipping Norton Town Clerk's Office, 1566 lease of manor; TNA, SC6/HENVII/491.

33 Gloucester Cathedral Library, Register C part 1 (Thomas Braunche), ff.45v-6v.

CHAPTER 2

THE AGE OF HENRY CORNISH, 1540—1660

REFORMATION AND RELIGIOUS PROPERTY

The early stages of the Protestant Reformation were uneventful at Chipping Norton. Cold Norton Priory had always been a small religious house, and after it closed in 1507 the priory's land in the town fields was given to Brasenose College at Oxford and continued to be farmed by local tenants as before. New religious ideas must have circulated, but even in the later years of Henry VIII's reign parishioners' wills show continued devotion to the gilded image of St George and the lights burning on side-altars and before the rood in the parish church. Prayers for the souls of the departed were also highly valued, and houses and cottages were bequeathed to the Trinity guild to pay for annual commemorations for years to come.[1]

The accession of Edward VI in 1547 brought sudden change. Within a year, Parliament had legislated to abolish chantries and religious guilds and to appropriate all their property for the Crown. Four of Chipping Norton's priests were dismissed, the plate and vestments of the three chantries were seized, and all of the land and housing given by townspeople for prayers and charitable purposes became royal property. After nearly a century as the forum and meeting-place of the town's leading citizens, the Trinity guild closed and the Guildhall was put up for sale. The grammar school in Church Street was saved after the townspeople petitioned for its survival; other market towns including Burford and Banbury made very similar but unsuccessful pleas for their own schools, and it is not clear why Chipping Norton's school was one of only two in Oxfordshire to survive. Perhaps the lady of the manor, Dame Elizabeth Hoby, used her influence. In July 1548 the priest who had taught at Chipping Norton, Hamlet Malban, was reappointed as schoolmaster with a stipend of £6 a year. Many of his successors were vicars of Chipping Norton who doubled as masters of the grammar school, living at the school in Church Street as there was no vicarage house until the later seventeenth century.[2]

Sales of confiscated Church property began immediately and in March 1549 all three 'mansions' where the chantry priests had lived were sold to London officials and gentlemen. In May commissioners arrived to take a second survey of goods belonging to the parish church, prompting fears of their confiscation as well. Many communities quietly removed items from the church and sold or entrusted them to parishioners for safekeeping, and in 1558 Edward Phillips wrote in his will, 'I give to the church of Chipping Norton all that they owe me … and all that I bought of the church it is my will it be restored to the church again'. June 1549 brought Cranmer's new Prayer Book, which replaced the familiar Latin Mass with church services in English. Protests in the north of England, in East Anglia and the West Country escalated into rebellion, and in July 1549 men took up arms in Oxfordshire. The local rising was short-lived but it had a devastating impact on Chipping Norton, where the rebels briefly set up camp. Lord Grey of Wilton and his forces soon caught up with them, probably near Enslow Bridge over the River Cherwell, and killed or captured many while the rest fled. Parish clergy were singled out by the government as ringleaders of the rising and among those executed was the vicar of Chipping Norton, Henry Joyce, who was hanged from the church tower. Whether he had in fact incited rebellion, or had merely offered help to the rebels camped in his parish, is unknown.[3]

Not surprisingly, there was no sign at Chipping Norton of any further opposition to official policy on worship under Edward or his sisters Queen Mary and Queen Elizabeth, and we can assume that the parish made the required changes in the church. Side-altars, images including the statue of St George, and the lights burning before them were all removed and the chapel of the Holy Trinity guild was destroyed. Under Elizabeth, rood screens came down and the main altar was replaced by a communion table in the nave. As time passed a new generation grew up with Protestant teaching and worship, and memories of Catholic customs gradually faded. There were few Catholic recusants at Chipping Norton and the town settled into the moderate Puritanism common throughout north Oxfordshire.

Meanwhile, sales by the Crown of Church and guild property continued. In December 1549 two London gentlemen bought the Guildhall itself with

21 Stairs in Chipping Norton's parish church which once led up to the rood loft, before the destruction of the rood screen at the Reformation. Above the staircase is one of the empty niches which had held statues of saints.

four houses and a garden from the guild lands, and more property from the chantry of St Mary. Further sales were recorded in 1550 and 1553. Most items were probably sold on immediately to local people taking advantage of this opportunity. Until its dissolution, the guild had held property to support its almshouse and the grammar school, but now there was no organisation to own buildings on behalf of the town community. The townspeople of Chipping Norton therefore adopted a legal device used in other towns and appointed 'feoffees' or trustees to hold property for common purposes. In 1562 the Guildhall was conveyed by Anthony Ashfield of the Heythrop gentry family, whose parents had been guild members, to four leading townsmen 'with the consent of the most part of the substantial and honest men of the town', and the upper room became known as Chipping Norton's 'town hall'.[4]

Ashfield had also bought chantry property in Church Street. Before his death in 1562 he sold to William Averell of Chipping Norton two large houses on the south side of the street. One of these was bought from Averell in 1572 by a group of townsmen and part of it was used to enlarge the school, while the adjoining house, formerly the chantry house of St John, was purchased in 1590 by another group of trustees to provide rent for the maintenance of the schoolmaster 'to teach and instruct the children and scholars of all the inhabitants of the town of Chipping Norton freely, without paying any thing therefor, in the Latin tongue'. Had Anthony Ashfield bought these important buildings with the intention of returning them to the town, or was it a shrewd investment? He was also the purchaser of the George Inn, formerly owned by the chantry of St James, which he quickly sold on to a private buyer. Perhaps he intended to combine profit with principle.[5]

The properties lost at the Reformation were not all large buildings, for the guild and chantries had also been given cottages throughout the town. A collection of twelve cottages formerly owned by the guild, and another ten once held by the chantry of St Mary, passed through many hands and were eventually bought by Sir Anthony Cope of Hanwell and his brother Sir Walter. Both brothers died in 1614 and their property was inherited by Sir Anthony's son, Sir William Cope of Hanwell. The Copes were leading Puritans who spoke out in Parliament for reform of the Church of England, but they were also deeply involved in syndicates speculating in former Church lands bought from James I. Their property at Chipping Norton was not limited to cottages, for the substantial fifteenth-century house at no. 8 Market Street was sold by Sir William Cope in 1618, and this house too may once have belonged to a chantry or the guild.[6]

A group of twelve cottages was bequeathed in 1650 in the will of Henry Cornish, the wealthy mercer who built Chipping Norton's almshouses, and this may well be the same collection of former guild properties since Cornish had bought them (with other cottages in the town) from Sir William Cope. Cornish left instructions that the cottages were to be let at fixed rents to 'persons of the poorer sort' who were 'honest, peaceable and religious', chosen by the Corporation. Although Cornish's original cottages no longer exist and have been replaced by others, including a Victorian group of four known as Cock's Row in Horsefair, the charity continues to the present day. The old name 'King's Hold' for the charitable cottages dates from the early seventeenth century; one of them stood on the site of no. 72 West Street and in documents of 1628 and 1652 we find 'King's Holding', 'King's Lands' and 'the King's Hold tenements', all referring to the period when these former guild lands were owned by the Crown.[7]

MARKETS AND CRAFTSMEN

The basis of Chipping Norton's economy from the sixteenth to the nineteenth centuries was its long-established role as a market town. England's international trade in wool gradually declined, and was replaced in some towns by the manufacture of woollen cloth. Nearby Witney's clothiers and blanket-makers prospered, but Chipping Norton had no fast-flowing river to power fulling-mills, which were essential for a profitable cloth industry. Instead the town offered a variety of trades using the raw materials of the area – leather from cattle and other hides, malt from local barley, wheat, timber and stone – as well as services for the local community and for travellers passing through. Buyers and sellers from the fertile marlstone and limestone region to the east met those from the Cotswold upland villages and the farmers of the Evenlode valley at Chipping Norton's market each Wednesday. Markets were competitive and needed to offer good facilities such as a spacious market place with separate areas for stalls and livestock, efficient administration of weights and measures and the resolution of disputes. 'The inhabitants of Chipping Norton did build the market house and ever since repair the same… the bellman of the town hath received the toll of corn and grain, [and] doth stand under the eaves of the market house',

22 A pillar from the market house replaced by the Town Hall.

said a witness in 1607. Later illustrations (e.g. Fig. 1) show different market houses in use during the eighteenth and early nineteenth centuries, all of them open-sided structures with either a gabled or a flat roof supported on pillars, to provide shelter for perishable foodstuffs such as butter. The last market house stood on the site of the present Town Hall until 1842 and a section of one of its pillars is preserved close by. The ground floor of the Guildhall was also used for selling. Its doorway suggests that it was enclosed rather than open-sided, and probably provided small booths for traders from outside the town. In 1612 the ground floor was leased to a baker, George Carter, who presumably rented out the booths.[8]

Crafts practised in the town catered to the everyday needs of the local population. Numerous cordwainers (shoemakers), glovers and one or two saddlers and horse-collar makers made use of locally produced leather, and chandlers rendered down animal carcasses to make tallow for candles. Chipping Norton's weavers, tuckers and shearmen probably worked for Witney clothiers, while tailors made use of the finished cloth. The town had several blacksmiths in the seventeenth century including one at the north end of Middle Row, another above the Blue Boar at the top of Goddard's Lane and one at no. 4 West Street next to the Swan. Craftsmen in wood included carpenters, joiners, coopers, wheelwrights and ploughwrights, and masons, slatters and glaziers represented the building trades. Butchers and bakers were the main food suppliers and in the early seventeenth century many of the wealthier townsmen did some malting. Most of these crafts did not need specialised premises and they have left little trace in Chipping Norton's buildings. The seventeenth-century house with its outbuildings was a flexible space, and rooms, attics and barns could be put to many uses.

Industrial activity could be found throughout the town. We can imagine the sounds and smells of soap-boiling and tallow-chandling on the south corner of Middle Row and at West End Farm, a carpenter's sawpit in New Street, a bakery at the south end of High Street and brewing at the large inns. Added to this were the sounds of transport with the rumble of carts and the clop of horses' hooves. Horses were grazed on the Common below the town, and all the larger houses had stables. On the site of no. 2 Church Street was the horsepool, fed by one of the springs arising above Spring Street, where horses were washed and watered. On market days many more horses were brought into the town by traders and customers and the inns provided temporary stabling. The Swan in 1744 was said to have 'good stables that will contain 100 horses'.[9]

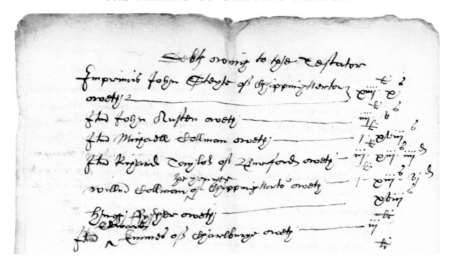

23 Debts for leather owed to Thomas Letch at his death in 1634 by customers in Chipping Norton, Burford and Charlbury. (OHC, MS Wills Oxon 41/3/38: inventory of Thomas Letch 1634)

Leather-working had been important to Chipping Norton's economy since the medieval period and tanning became more prominent as the wool trade declined. This was an industry requiring vacant land and a good water supply, as the hides were soaked for many months in a series of pits containing solutions of lime, dog dung and ground oak bark. The tannery in Church Lane was owned in the sixteenth century by the Henshaws, from whom it passed by marriage to the Letch family from Hornton near Banbury. John Letch died in 1628 leaving goods worth more than £600, including leather and hides worth £360, calf skins, tan vats and two mills for shredding bark. His son Thomas sold leather over a wide area. The Letch family operated the tannery until about 1712 and were succeeded by the Norgroves. This tannery survived into the nineteenth century and must have contributed a distinctive smell to the northern end of Spring Street.[10]

A second large tannery was established in the seventeenth century adjacent to the farmhouse of the Brayne family at no. 37 West Street (now known as Rowell's House). The land 'which is now a tanhouse built upon' was bought by the vicar of Chipping Norton, John Norgrove, who came from a leather-working family in Shropshire, and after his death in 1659 the tannery descended in the Norgrove family. There were other tanners working at Chipping Norton on a smaller scale. Their tanpits are likely to have been along Spring Street and West Street to take advantage of the water supply below the spring line.[11]

SHOPS AND INNS

Many of the town's wealthiest inhabitants were engaged principally in trade rather than manufacture. Drapers, ironmongers, haberdashers and especially mercers were well represented in the town's social and economic elite. When Chipping Norton acquired a charter in 1607, six of the thirteen men named as the first burgesses were mercers or woollendrapers. Samuel Harris, a haberdasher, had more than one shop in 1616 and his stock consisted largely of hats. Richard Berry was described as both a mercer and a linendraper but like most tradesmen he carried a wide range of goods for sale; in 1626 his shop was equipped with a spice mortar and pestle, and he sold ironmongery items such as nails, slate pins and rakes. Shops offered consumers the convenience of trade on six days a week rather than a weekly market, and they also provided credit. The shops of the large retailers were located around the market place.[12]

Probate inventories drawn up after a death to value the goods of the deceased show us some of Chipping Norton's shops and their contents. In a collection of sixty-two inventories for the more affluent inhabitants between 1580 and 1650, more than 40 per cent listed a room called a 'shop'. Many sold a variety of wares, like Mark Preston's mercery shop in 1640 which displayed everyday fabrics such as bolster ticking and 'aproning' as well as finer cloths, grocery items such as honey, sugar, soap and starch, brown paper and parchment, and haberdashery including buttons, garters and laces. Joan Carrick in 1612 sold earthenware pots and dishes from premises that included both a shop and a 'room within the shop', and her cellar held further stocks of earthenware. Many shops were used as workshops as well as retail premises. Shoemakers' shops usually contained ready-made shoes and boots for sale in addition to the leather, tallow, thread, lasts and tools for making them. John Hyatt, a carpenter, had six pairs of hames (part of a draught horse's collar), 400 elm boards, three ladders and ten pairs of rafters in his 'shop' in 1624. Even a yeoman farmer or an innkeeper might have a room called a shop, and it seems that the name was a flexible label for any space intended for transactions with customers. The inventories do not specify the position of each room but a shop would normally be accessible from the street at the front of the house. Most appear to have been within the ground-floor house plan with first-floor chambers above, as in Alice Deacon's house in 1600 with a 'chamber over the shop and hall'.[13]

24 Items from the inventory of Mark Preston's mercer's shop, including glasses for examining urine, brass scales, cloth at various prices, coifs and brown thread. (OHC, MS Wills Oxon 51/3/27: inventory of Mark Preston 1640)

Henry Cornish (c.1576-1650), the leading tradesman at Chipping Norton in the first half of the seventeenth century, was a mercer, as were his father and his elder brother. Henry was an energetic and forceful businessman and at his death it was said that he had £1,200 in money and goods and £700 in farm stock, owned eight yardlands (about 160 acres) of arable land, and had acquired at least eight houses and many cottages in Chipping Norton as well as property at Stow-on-the-Wold. He had a house in High Street, although in his last years he lived at no. 5 West Street. Henry and his first wife Elizabeth had twelve children but almost all died in infancy, and their only two children to survive to adulthood both died young. Without any direct descendants to inherit his wealth, and perhaps also prompted by his Puritan beliefs, Cornish provided for his wider family and founded generous charities in Chipping Norton. Cottages were to be let to poor townspeople at low rents, funds were established for annual doles of bread, clothing and money, and Cornish provided for an annual dinner at his own inn, the White Hart, for his successors in the Corporation. His name lives on at Chipping Norton and his charities still benefit the town.[14]

25 The Cornish almshouses, Church Street.

26 Plaque
on one of the
almshouse
gables:
'The Work and
Gift of Henry
Cornish Gent
1640'.

In 1640, ten years before he died, Henry Cornish bought a plot in Church Street and built a row of almshouses for eight poor widows. Church Street is on a steep slope, but the site was levelled and the almshouses are set back from the street to be seen as a complete row, unlike cottages in the town. It is likely that the founder was closely involved in their design and his name is recorded on a plaque. Carved over the gateway is the admonition 'Remember the poor'.

Tudor and Stuart England saw a steady increase in internal trade and travel. Whether on foot or horseback, in one of the new horse-drawn coaches or a carrier's cart, a constant stream of people and goods moved up and down the country, and a town like Chipping Norton was well placed to serve their needs. The 'great road from London to Worcester' followed several routes, one of which brought travellers through the market place from London Road to New Street, and onwards to Stow and Evesham, which in 1538 claimed 'a great thoroughfare into Wales'. The 'London way' heading north to the east of Chipping Norton was also the main road from Oxford to Stratford and the West Midlands. Long-distance and local travellers were customers for the town's shops, blacksmiths and alehouses, and the growth of travel also encouraged the opening of inns.[15]

Already well established by 1500, the White Hart at no. 16 High Street maintained its position as the town's leading inn. In 1603 it was bought by Henry Cornish and the building's fine seventeenth-century fire-surrounds, traces of wall-painting, panelling and stone vaulted cellar all demonstrate the investment of Cornish and his successors. A second large inn, the Talbot, had opened at nos 3-4 High Street (now replaced by the Co-op) by 1591. The proprietor was Thomas Rainsford, gentleman, probably a younger son of the gentry family of Great Tew; the landed gentry lived on their country estates but a younger son had to make his own way in the world. The White Hart and the Talbot both held licences for selling wine. A third inn, the Swan, was in business by 1608 just outside the market place at no. 2 West Street.[16]

The opening of the Crown & Cushion Inn at no. 23 High Street can also be dated to the first half of the seventeenth century. The building had been the 'mansion house' of Edmund Hutchins (d.1602) who was both a wealthy descendant of one of Chipping Norton's medieval woolmen and the nephew of Sir Thomas Pope, treasurer of the Court of Augmentations and the founder of Trinity College, Oxford. The house was bought from Hutchins's heirs about 1620 by Robert Mayor, who opened it as an inn called the Crown. The name had changed to the Katherine Wheel by the 1660s, perhaps in deference to republican sentiments during the Civil War, but later reverted to the Crown or the Crown & Cushion. In the records of hearth tax paid in 1662 the inns can be identified as some of the largest buildings in the town: fourteen hearths at the White Hart, twelve at the Swan, eleven at the Talbot and eight at the Katherine Wheel.[17]

FARMING AND FARMHOUSES

Facilities such as shops and inns were characteristically urban, and visitors to Chipping Norton in the early seventeenth century observing its closely built-up streets, tiled roofs instead of thatch, and the throng of people on market day would be in no doubt that they had arrived in a town. Nevertheless, farming was integral to life in country towns and urban buildings could accommodate livestock, crops and equipment. Between 1580 and 1660 more than 20 per cent of the men at Chipping Norton for whom a will or probate inventory survives described themselves as husbandmen or yeomen and were full-time farmers, both rearing sheep and cattle and growing crops, principally wheat and barley. Craftsmen often kept a few animals such as poultry or a cow to supplement their income, and innkeepers and maltsters kept pigs behind their properties and fed them on the mash from malting and brewing. Many townspeople derived a significant part of their livelihood from farming, and inventories list outbuildings such as barns, sheep-houses, dairies, stables and haylofts. Inside the house, a room might be described as a cheese chamber or a malt chamber, and in some homes produce could be found stored all over the house – wool and hemp to be spun, malt, honey, cheeses, flitches of bacon, feathers, flour and grain. In 1590 the possessions of Eleanor Simkins, widow of a prosperous husbandman living in one of the High Street houses, were listed in her probate inventory. She owned ploughs, carts and harrows, an ox-house for her three oxen, a stable and hayloft for two horses, six pigs, two dairy cows, a barn containing barley, and a sheep-house for her flock of fifty-nine sheep; wood was stacked in the 'lower court' and at the back gate, and above the back lane (Albion Street) was a little rick of corn.[18]

The buildings at Chipping Norton dating from the first half of the seventeenth century suggest that large farmers were prospering. Three or four substantial stone houses were built or re-built in this period in West Street,

27 West End Farmhouse, West Street.

28 College Place, West Street. (Photograph: P.S. Spokes)

where the outskirts of the town offered large plots for spacious farmyards. The eighteenth-century Rowell's House at no. 37 West Street incorporates a barrel-vaulted cellar and a re-used mullioned window that are probably survivals from an early seventeenth-century house. West End Farmhouse at no. 43 West Street, and College Place on the other side of the street a little further south, are both two-storey six-bay houses of the early seventeenth century with the new features that were transforming domestic life: chimneystacks and enclosed fireplaces to remove the smoke, staircases and first-floor chambers, and glazed windows. At no. 44 West Street is another former farmhouse whose main range could date from the early or late seventeenth century with a possible lobby-entry plan. It follows rural styles, turning its back on the street so the main entrance was through the farmyard, and on one corner a stair tower houses a stone spiral staircase which originally climbed all the way from the cellars to the attic.

In the town, another seventeenth-century farmhouse is now divided into three as nos 30-34 Spring Street. Yet another new farmhouse was built at nos 63-65 New Street, probably by William Diston, one of the first burgesses and brother-in-law of Henry Cornish. When Diston died in 1626 he left two yardlands (40 acres), 160 sheep, a small dairy herd and ten bushels of malt, and his home was comfortably furnished with court cupboards in the parlour and the chamber above it, a looking-glass and needlework cushions.[19]

HOMES AND HOUSEHOLDS

Most people in Chipping Norton lived in older houses, adapted and furnished to suit their needs, and probate inventories drawn up between 1580 and 1650 provide a glimpse of their homes and possessions. The main room in every house at this period was the hall. From the presence of fire-shovels and bellows it is evident that most halls had a hearth, often the only one in the house. In medieval houses the hall had been open to the roof, and the insertion of a ceiling and creation of first-floor chambers above the hall was one of the innovations introduced in the sixteenth and seventeenth centuries. Towns were generally at the forefront of change and by 1600 many houses in Chipping Norton, perhaps a majority, had first-floor rooms. The large High Street house of Eleanor Simkins, already mentioned, had a hall, parlour, kitchen, buttery and shop on the ground floor with chambers above the hall, parlour and shop. But the inventories also show much smaller houses such as cottages in the poorer areas of Spring Street or West Street where life was less comfortable. The living space of William Hayes, a slatter and small farmer who died in 1587, consisted of a 'hall house' where the family prepared, cooked and ate their meals. The single chamber with two bedsteads and a truckle bed was probably a first-floor room inserted at one end of the hall and accessed by the ladders listed in the inventory. Hayes lived here with his wife and two young daughters but with space at a premium his two sons had already left home. His furniture and household goods were valued at just £2 10s 4d. There must have been many households like this in the town, as well as poorer families whose belongings were not worth the cost of an inventory.[20]

Listings of pots and pans indicate that in at least half of the households described in the inventories, cooking took place in the hall. A kitchen, mentioned in just under half the documents, was used for storage of large dishes and for processes such as salting meat and brewing. Many kitchens contained a 'furnace', which was an oven or boiler. Only one inventory from this period shows a house with a chamber over its kitchen, and it appears that kitchens were additions to medieval houses, either detached outbuildings or lean-to extensions. In 1587 Thomas Walter, a husbandman, bequeathed 'the hall house and chambers' to his wife whereas 'my kitchen containing a bay of housing' was left to his son.[21]

The other ground-floor room commonly mentioned between 1580 and 1650 was a parlour. Just under half of these households had a parlour, mainly the more affluent, and the name appears more frequently from the 1630s onwards. Its function varied from a general living space with cooking facilities to a ground-floor sleeping room or a well-furnished room for entertaining. An exceptionally detailed inventory of 1639 for James Henshaw, a wealthy maltster who lived at the south end of High Street in the corner of the market place, portrays his parlour as a heated room of considerable comfort and display. Henshaw's 'high bedstead' with green bed-curtains and valance stood there, and his clothing was kept in the parlour with personal possessions such as two swords, a bible and a tobacco box. While cooking for the household was done in the hall, food was served in the parlour on platters and dishes that were stored in a court cupboard with six silver spoons. There were two tables and the seating included a 'great joined chair', two little chairs and a child's chair as well as seven joined stools, with fourteen cushions. Picture frames suggest that pictures hung on the walls and there were curtains at the windows. The room reflected the status of its owner, and Henshaw probably entertained customers as well as friends in his parlour.[22]

The chambers above ground-floor halls and parlours were mostly used as bedrooms, with truckle beds beneath bedsteads for children and servants, but also as general storage rooms for furniture, household linen and trade goods. Most chambers had no fireplace in this period.

THE FABRIC OF HOUSES

While inventories offer snapshots of homes at a single moment in time, there is much less evidence about the construction of Chipping Norton's buildings or the constant process of refurbishment, repair and replacement. Walter Thomas, the first town clerk, estimated in 1624 that over the previous twenty years he had spent the large sum of £40 on 'building, repairing and amending' his house at no. 1 Market Place. The east-west range at the back of Bitter & Twisted on the south-east corner of Middle Row was rebuilt in the seventeenth century, and heavy moulded beams from the sixteenth century can be seen at no. 9 Middle Row (Whistlers) and at the King's Arms in

29 Early seventeenth-century range of the Chequers, Spring Street, from the south.

West Street which was then a private house. The only surviving buildings at Chipping Norton known to have been newly constructed between 1600 and 1660, in addition to the farmhouses already mentioned, were the north-south range of the Chequers (then a private house) in Spring Street, where tree-ring dating gives a felling date for a purlin of 1613–18, and Henry Cornish's almshouses of 1640 in Church Street. Others have disappeared in later rebuilding, such as the two seventeenth-century cottages refronted c.1780 as one house at no. 15 Market Place. The town had two or three stonemasons and slatters in this period as well as carpenters and sawyers. Most building craftsmen were not well off and supplemented their incomes by farming, and their small numbers suggest that demand for their skills was limited.[23]

Interior updating would have provided more work than new building. Moulded stone 'Tudor' fireplaces, in fashion from the fifteenth to the seventeenth centuries, have been found at the Fox, no. 9 Market Street, no. 10 Middle Row, and College Place. A glazier, William Knowles, was working by 1608 at Chipping Norton, where glass had already replaced medieval shutters in many buildings: in 1592 a drunken crowd 'from house to house along the streets did break down and spoil divers and sundry of their neighbours' glass windows'. For those who could afford it, panelling was a fashionable and decorative form of insulation, and seventeenth-century panelling survives at no. 65 New Street, the White Hart and the house now called the Manor House. The construction of staircases for access to new upper-floor chambers was also popular. In 1631 Thomas Turner, a tailor, left detailed instructions for the division of his house between his son and his widow. His son's share was the shop and the chamber above it, and a buttery, while his widow received the hall and chambers over the hall and entry, 'and if my son Christopher do find that her going up and down to be a trouble through the chamber over the shop I do enjoin him to make her a pair of stairs in the hall'.[24]

Large houses could also be divided to create smaller units for multiple occupation. The division in 1609 of one of the houses in the 'nether row' (Market Street), described as an 'ancient messuage', was meticulously documented. Edward Dawson, a shepherd, received a long lease of the shop and parlour with the chambers above them and a kitchen adjoining the parlour, with half the backside and garden; Arthur More, a tailor, was allocated the hall and the chamber above it, two bays of a cross wing and the other half of the backside and garden, and the two tenants were to share the entry. Later leases of the property show further subdivision with single rooms rented to widows, shoemakers, a shepherd and a woolwinder.[25] The large fifteenth-

30 Tudor stone fireplace photographed by Frank Packer in the early 1900s at no. 10 Middle Row.

31 Early seventeenth-century panelling at the Manor House, West Street.

century houses along Market Street were by now old-fashioned and the development of Middle Row had cut them off from the market place. It was no longer profitable to rebuild them, and it would be easier to find tenants for small units than for a large house. The same process took place in Spring Street where many houses and cottages belonged to landlords who lived elsewhere in the town. Henry Cornish owned two houses just south of Church Lane, and by 1618 one of these had been divided into two with a partition wall of wattle and plaster, and both units were let to labourers.[26] The poorest inhabitants of Chipping Norton in the seventeenth century are almost invisible as none of the records of poor relief have survived, but there was evidently a demand for cheap housing.

The scarcity of new construction in the town centre in the sixteenth and early seventeenth centuries might suggest that this was a period of economic decline at Chipping Norton. The international wool trade no longer brought wealth to the town to be spent on building. Edmund Hutchins, the town's richest Elizabethan inhabitant and the descendant of a woolman, moved away to become a country gentleman on his Gloucestershire estate. The period could, however, be characterised as one of transition as Chipping Norton adjusted to a more limited role. The economy of a market town was closely linked to the prosperity of its hinterland, and the construction of five or six new farmhouses in this period does not suggest that agricultural incomes were in decline. The population of Chipping Norton was growing in the sixteenth and seventeenth centuries and the town attracted immigrants from the countryside. Baptisms recorded in the parish registers exceeded burials in every decade from the 1570s to the 1660s, and the town's hilltop location and clean water supply minimised the impact of disease. In 1662, 158 households were assessed for hearth tax, slightly more than at Burford but fewer than Witney, and the town's population probably stood close to 1,000.

The tradesmen and craftsmen who made up the town's elite were prosperous enough, and the lists of contents of their houses show that expenditure was being directed to comfort, convenience and decoration rather than new building. It is interesting to note that Henry Cornish did not use his wealth to build an impressive new house, as his predecessors in the fifteenth century or his successors in the eighteenth would have done. No probate inventory listing his possessions has survived but we can assume that he lived in comfort. Instead of construction, Cornish invested in land, agriculture, the White Hart and a large collection of urban properties, and left his charities and the almshouses as his monument.

Looking back from 1660, the town had survived the loss of its medieval wool trade. It had also gained its legal independence in 1607 when the townsmen defied their new lord of the manor, Michael Chadwell, and successfully applied for a charter of incorporation, and the Corporation was finally able to purchase the lordship of the manor for itself in 1668.[27] A century or more of limited investment in buildings meant that by the later seventeenth century there was ample scope – and probably a pressing need – for the reconstruction which was to change the face of the town, as we shall see in the next chapter.

Notes to Chapter 2

1 *VCH Oxon.* ii. 96-7; OHC, MS Wills Oxon 178.26 (will of Joan Mitton 1530); 178.131 (will of Isabel Tanty 1538).

2 R. Graham (ed.), *Chantry Certificates* (ORS 1, 1919), 20-2, 45-7, 55-6.

3 *Cal. Pat. 1548-9*, 192, 414-15; OHC, MS Wills Oxon 181.273 (will of Edward Phillips 1558); K. Halliday, 'New light on 'the commotion time' of 1549: the Oxfordshire rising', *Historical Research*, 82 (2009), 1-26.

4 *Cal. Pat. 1549-51*, 82-4, 283; *1553*, 246; CNM, 1842 abstract of title to Guildhall.

5 *Report of Commissioners concerning Charities and Education of the Poor* (1815-39), vol. xxvi, 257; Bodl. MS. D.D. Dawkins, C.9.B.5/4.

6 Hampshire Record Office, Cope MSS, 43M48/209-10; for the Copes' financial dealings see A.F. Upton, *Sir Arthur Ingram c.1565-1642* (1961), 23-7, 39; M. Prestwich, *Cranfield: Politics and Profits under the Early Stuarts* (1966), 32, 145-6; CNM, summary of deeds for 8 Market Street.

7 TNA, PROB 11/214/314 (will of Henry Cornish 1650); E. Meades, *History of Chipping Norton* (2nd edn 1984), 57-8; D. Eddershaw, *Chipping Norton, the Story of a Market Town* (2006), 60 note 2; BNC, BO 522 Chipping Norton terriers, (1628) no.1; (1652) nos 1-3.

8 TNA, STAC 8/162/7; CNM, 1612 decree re Guildhall; D. Clark, 'The shop within?: an analysis of the architectural evidence for medieval shops', *Architectural History*, 43 (2000), 63.

9 *London Evening Post*, 10 Jan. 1744.

10 R. Thomson, 'Leather manufacture in the post-medieval period with special reference to Northamptonshire', *Post-medieval Archaeology*, 15 (1981), 161-70; OHC, MS Wills Oxon 139/1/32 (inventory of John Letch 1628); 41/3/38 (inventory of Thomas Letch 1634).

11 TNA, PROB 11/288 (will of John Norgrove 1659).

12 OHC, MS Wills Oxon 30/2/24 (will and inventory of Samuel Harris 1616); TNA, PROB 11/150 (will of Richard Berry 1626).

13 OHC, MS Wills Oxon 51/3/27 (inventory of Mark Preston 1640); 11/4/12 (inventory of Joan Carrick 1612); 30/4/37 (inventory of John Hyatt 1624); 296/4/20 (inventory of Alice Deacon 1600).

14 TNA, PROB 11/214 (will of Henry Cornish 1650); TNA, C3/441/17.

15 H.B. Wheatley and E.W. Ashbee (eds), *The Particular Description of England, 1588, by William Smith* (1879), 71; *VCH Worcs.* ii. 126.

16 TNA, C3/385/10; Simons, 'White Hart Hotel, Chipping Norton', *Oxoniensia*, 70 (2005), 312, 316; TNA, STAC 5/C32/37; R. Taylor (ed.), *Calendar of the Court Books of Woodstock 1607-22* (ORS 65, 2007), 8, 17.

17 TNA, PROB 11/104 (will of Edmund Hutchins 1604); TNA, C2/JasI/M16/57; TNA, E179/255/3; information on wine licences kindly supplied by Jeremy Gibson.

18 OHC, MS Wills Oxon 58/2/23 (inventory of Eleanor Simkins 1589).

19 OHC, MS Wills Oxon 17/4/20 (will and inventory of William Diston 1626).

20 OHC, MS Wills Oxon 58/2/23 (inventory of Eleanor Simkins 1589); 131/4/23 (will and inventory of William Hayes 1587).

21 OHC, MS Wills Oxon 69/1/47 (will of Thomas Walter 1587).

22 OHC, MS Wills Oxon 298/1/43a-b (inventory of James Henshaw 1639).

23 TNA, C 3/385/10.

24 TNA, C2/JasI/K3/33; TNA, STAC 5/C65/17; OHC, MS Wills Oxon 66/1/34 (will of Thomas Turner 1632).

25 OHC, O12/26D/1-4; Bodl. MS. Ch. Oxon. 2766-7.

26 CNM, summary of deeds for 53 Spring Street.

27 TNA, E 179/255/3; Eddershaw, *Chipping Norton*, 47-53.

CHAPTER 3

REBUILDING THE TOWN, 1660–1750

CHIPPING NORTON survived the Civil War and Interregnum with its buildings and its economy largely intact, although the period had been difficult and dangerous for everyone. The main roads had brought troops from both armies through the town with the inevitable looting, billeting of soldiers, disease and violence. Taxation was heavy, and wealth tended to attract attention: both Henry Cornish and his nephew William Diston were held for ransom by troops at Oxford. However, there were no pitched battles and the physical damage seems to have been minor.

An indirect result of the war was the fall of the Chadwell family as major landholders at Chipping Norton. When Michael Chadwell sold the lordship of the manor in 1608 he had kept most of its property, including the fifteenth-century manor house in New Street. His grandson Michael, already struggling with family debts, took up arms for Charles I and after the war had to pay heavy fines. Eventually the financial burden became too great and in 1652 he sold the 'mansion house' and most of his land to John Crispe, a young attorney. The Crispe family replaced the Chadwells as owners of much of the south side of New Street, and John Crispe paid tax for his nine-hearth house there in 1662.[1]

FARMERS AND MALTSTERS

Farming in north-west Oxfordshire remained the basis of local prosperity, producing crops and livestock to sell, and customers with money to spend, at Chipping Norton's Wednesday markets and at the seven annual fairs.

32 Sheep-pens in the High Street in 1913.

On market days sheep-pens were set up along the central section of High Street, and the Corporation as lord of the manor granted leases for use of the street to the owner or occupant of each house. In front of properties at the north and south ends of High Street, licences granted the right to rent space to stallholders. These sheepground and stallage leases survive from 1668 and are a useful source of information about the occupants of High Street and Middle Row.[2]

The larger farmers at Chipping Norton and Over Norton still had flocks of 100 or more sheep and many also kept small dairy herds. Soil fertility was improved in the later seventeenth century by the introduction of nitrogen-fixing crops, particularly sainfoin, into the traditional rotations. Simon Trout of West End Farmhouse, for instance, had 'sointfine seed' stored in a garret in 1702. By the early eighteenth century a smaller proportion of the town's population was engaged in agriculture than a century earlier, and those who farmed were generally operating on a larger scale. The ownership of land was still widely distributed, however, and many of the town's tradesmen owned closes or parcels of arable land as an investment and leased them to farmers. Every Chipping Norton householder had the right to graze two horses or cows on the Common. Livestock were still a common sight in the town as many houses had stables and pigsties at the rear and butchers' slaughterhouses were located close to their shops, but almost all of the large farmhouses were now on the outskirts.[3]

The thin limestone soil was well suited to growing barley, and by the early 1700s malting had developed into a significant industry. Documentary evidence shows malthouses, kilnhouses and garners (grain stores) at several properties in the town, owned by both full-time and part-time maltsters. Behind no. 1 Market Place, for instance, the home until 1674 of the town clerk, William Thomas, his premises included a malthouse and a garner chamber, kiln chamber and malt chamber. A large malthouse was built just behind no. 65 New Street, possibly by the maltster Josiah Diston (d.1721) who lived in the 'church lane', later known as Diston's Lane; the farmhouse in New Street had a kitchen or brewhouse 'situate under the barley and malt garners' of the malthouse.[4] None of the town's early malthouse buildings are now recognisable but it is likely that some of their fabric survives in walls and outbuildings. Because malt was bulky to transport, most malting centres were towns with access to a navigable river, particularly Henley, which shipped large quantities of malt down the Thames to London's breweries. Chipping Norton's maltsters had no such advantage. Perhaps, like the Burford maltsters, they carted malt to Radcot Bridge to be loaded onto barges. A case heard in 1720 shows malt travelling even further overland, when Edward Parker, who rented a malthouse in Horsefair, joined other maltsters to send a large consignment of malt to Oxford and then all the way to Abingdon for shipping. Their malt was sold on arrival in London for £300, but unfortunately the lighter conveying it to the purchaser's brewery was sunk by 'a sudden tempest arising on ye River Thames' and most of the cargo was lost.[5] Not all the malt manufactured at Chipping Norton travelled so far as there was also local demand from inns and large households which did their own brewing.

LEATHERWORKERS AND WEAVERS

Leather-working was another important contributor to Chipping Norton's economy. Many of the hides and skins came from the town's butchers who rented closes at the edge of the town where their animals grazed until being brought in for slaughter. Tanners, skinners and curriers processed the hides, and tallow-chandlers boiled down the carcasses. Different kinds of leather were used by saddlers, collarmakers, glovers and breeches-makers, and by the cordwainers or shoemakers who outnumbered all the other leather trades. The inventory of a glover, Richard Davis, in 1698 shows some of the diversity of processes and products. At the tanpits he had three horse hides and calf, sheep and lamb skins, as well as beaver skins and 'other cutting leather' at his shop, and gloves and breeches ready made.[6]

Among the wealthiest tanners in the early eighteenth century were members of the Norgrove family who eventually acquired both the large tanyards. The West Street tannery was inherited by Nehemiah Norgrove (d.1693), who lived in comfort at College Place as a farmer and tanner. His son John succeeded him, but when he died in 1719 leaving eight young children the tannery passed to trustees and eventually to John Brayne (d.1744), who already owned the adjacent farmhouse at no. 37 West Street. Brayne prospered as a tanner and it is likely that he was the builder of the smart new residence (now called Rowell's House) that replaced the family farmhouse. An advertisement in 1766 described it as 'an exceeding good sashed house' with 'every convenience that is necessary to make a house commodious'. In his will Brayne left land in Chipping Norton and Over Norton, 'my silver tankard, silver salts, spoons and all my plate' and a large bible. Both he and John Norgrove were members of the Presbyterian congregation at Chipping Norton, and both married daughters of John Collier, a dissenter and one of Witney's leading clothiers.[7]

Meanwhile John Norgrove's cousin, Nathan Norgrove (d.1725), operated the tannery in Church Lane. In the 1680s he lived in the house on the corner of Spring Street and Goddard's Lane, now part of the Chequers. His son John (d.1730) expanded the tanyard into a close at the bottom of Church Lane near the churchyard. John Norgrove's will mentions a house associated with the tannery and this may be the three-bay section of the house called The Elm adjacent to Church Lane, where the roof structure suggests an early eighteenth-century date. All three of John's sons died childless and the tannery and other family property was inherited by his daughter Mary and her husband Thomas Rouse, also a tanner. After Mary's death in 1755 Thomas Rouse retired from tanning and became a victualler, opening their house in Goddard's Lane as the Blue Anchor Inn, later re-named the Chequers.[8]

The early eighteenth century saw the first signs of a new industry at Chipping Norton, the manufacture of woollen cloth. The number of weavers and woolcombers was small, but now instead of working for clothiers elsewhere some of them were master-weavers who owned their looms and controlled the process of manufacture from the purchase of wool to the

33 Rowell's House, West Street.

marketing of finished cloth. A detailed inventory of the goods left by Samuel Blissard, a weaver who died in 1752, listed various grades of wool and yarn, seven looms and many pieces of cloth – mainly harrateens, a heavy linen and wool fabric used for bed-curtains – including some in London awaiting sale. Blissard's premises in Horsefair included his well-furnished home, his workshop and a 'comb shop' for combing wool. The Witts family of Witney who were leading wool-factors sent a representative to Chipping Norton to establish a branch in an area with excellent wool supplies. In 1729 Edward Witts bought the house at no. 5 Market Place (and subsequently the adjoining property to the north) and his young son Broome took up residence. Trading as both a mercer and a wool-factor, Broome Witts was an active member of the Corporation until the 1750s when he moved to London to set up business as a linendraper, leaving his son Edward in charge at Chipping Norton. In addition to the house and shop in Market Place, the Witts family bought the farmhouse at nos 30-34 Spring Street and Edward Witts had wool-rooms and warehouses there. A trade directory of 1784 lists four men at Chipping Norton manufacturing cloth: three produced harrateens and one made tilts or covers for wagons and barges, while Edward Witts dealt in wool. This was on a very small scale compared to Witney where more than fifty manufacturers were active, but Chipping Norton's cloth industry was destined to grow.[9]

SHOPS, INNS AND SERVICES

Occupations in the late seventeenth and early eighteenth centuries included those providing services to the local population and to visitors. The largest shopkeepers at Chipping Norton were still mercers, grocers and drapers. From the 1690s until 1729, no. 5 Market Place was the home and shop of Nehemiah Norgrove, younger son of Nehemiah Norgrove of the West Street tannery, who became a mercer. His business eventually failed and in 1729 he was declared bankrupt. An advertisement for the sale of his stock suggests that customers at Chipping Norton had access to luxury as well as everyday fabrics:

A large parcel of mercery, linen and woollen-drapery goods, viz. Persians, sarsnets, thread-satins, silk ditto, broad and narrow mantuas, shagreens, Florence satins; tabbies, silver ditto, damasks, brocades, tissues, Venetians, bed-damasks, velvet hoods, Dutch and Genoa black velvets, coloured ditto, paduseys, black mantuas, lutestrings, alamores, figur'd Turkies, crapes, poplins, dunjars, calamancoes, scarlet camblets, plods, stuffs, &c.

Chipping Norton also offered haberdashers (selling hats), tailors, a milliner, an upholsterer, ironmongers and 'tin men', and clock and watchmakers.[10]

Services available in the town included a growing community of medical practitioners, from apothecaries to barber surgeons and physicians. Otherwise there were few professional men: the vicar, the rector of Heythrop who had no house in his own parish, the Presbyterian minister, the master of the grammar school, and one or two scriveners and lawyers including the town clerk. Chipping Norton was a community of tradesmen, and it had few resident gentlemen. As

34 Trade tokens (private coinage) issued in the 1660s by William Diston, owner of the White Hart, and by the mercer Henry Fawler.

the vicar commented in 1738 when asked about families of distinction in his parish, 'in market towns seldom any persons of note'. Social facilities were modest (a bowling green in Horsefair was mentioned in 1720) but gatherings of polite society, whether residents or visitors, took place in the large inns. Annual highlights were the horse race meetings held north-east of the town on the Heath near Chapel House. By the 1730s the Corporation was actively involved in the races. Owners had to enter their horses beforehand at the Guildhall, and were required to stable them at inns that had contributed towards the prize, the Town Plate. London newspapers advertised the meeting and announced 'a ball each night for the ladies'.[11]

Chipping Norton's inns and shops continued to benefit from the town's location on major long-distance routes and the popularity of coach travel. Travellers from London or Oxford on the highway to Worcester took the modern A44 north from Glympton through Enstone. At the Chipping Norton turn they had the choice to continue north-west past Little Rollright, as recommended in 1675 by John Ogilby – passing Chapel House, a well-known coaching inn at the edge of the parish – or to take the route through the town and rejoin the former road at Bourton on the Hill. Richard Blome's description of Chipping Norton in 1673 as 'a large but straggling town, yet well compacted about the market place' reflects the seventeenth-century traveller's view of the approaches via London Road or New Street, which were less densely occupied than the town centre. A stagecoach service stopped in Chipping Norton as early as 1654, and by 1683 the official postal service carried letters three times a week from London to Worcester and the West Midlands, serving Chipping Norton on the way. In 1730 and 1731 the highways from Glympton to Rollright and from Chapel on the Heath to Bourton on the Hill were two of the earliest roads in Oxfordshire to be turnpiked.[12]

The large inns on the upper side of the market were all flourishing. In 1675 the White Hart at no. 16 High Street was fashionably furnished and the inn housed a barber's shop equipped with a looking-glass, basins and a water-pot. The Talbot (nos 3–4 High Street, now replaced by the Co-op) in 1694 welcomed its guests to a Queen's Chamber with red serge furniture and leather chairs, a Worcester Chamber, and Great and Little Hereford Chambers with yellow bed-curtains. The other large coaching inn, the Swan at the corner of West Street, had a Club Room in 1713 for local society meetings.[13]

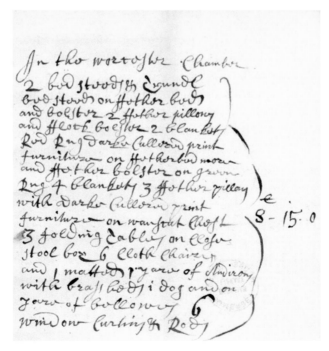

35 Inventory of the Worcester Chamber, one of the best rooms at the Talbot in 1694. The room had a fireplace, several windows, and two beds with 'dark coloured print' hangings and red and green rugs. (OHC, MS Wills Oxon 171/5/28: inventory of John Petyfer 1694)

Smaller inns and public houses were also doing well. The Blue Boar in Goddard's Lane, still a pub today, had been the home of Thomas Taylor (d.1673), a ropemaker, with his workshop at the back. His son William moved to High Street and opened the house in Goddard's Lane as the Blue Boar by 1708. Other inns trading in the first half of the eighteenth century included the Unicorn at no. 14 Market Place (now replaced by Sainsbury's), the Plough at no. 9 Market Street, the Black Horse below the Guildhall, the George at no. 4 New Street and the Blue Lion next door at no. 6, and many others. Two more which survive today opened soon after 1750: the Fox at no. 2 Market Place by 1768, and the Chequers in Goddard's Lane, originally called the Blue Anchor, after 1755.[14]

The King's Head (now King's Head Court) in New Street, which dates from the 1720s or early 1730s, represents a gentry family's attempt to capitalise on the inn trade. The old manor house had been inherited by Isabella Crispe (d.1725) and her son Thomas, one of whom refronted the mansion house and rebuilt the building at the western end of the manor house property as an inn. The King's Head has a striking nine-bay facade in the baroque style with giant order pilasters, sash windows and a cornice, a central carriage entrance and a stable block behind, obviously designed to

36 The King's Head, New Street.

compete with the coaching inns in the market place. Thomas Crispe sold his estate at Chipping Norton in 1744 so the venture may not have been profitable, and although the King's Head remained open until the 1860s it never posed any threat to the older establishments.[15]

REBUILDING THE TOWN

The records suggest that business was good for Chipping Norton's building craftsmen in this period. From the late seventeenth century onwards, and particularly after 1700, more masons, carpenters, slatters and glaziers are mentioned in documents, more of them owned property, and at death many had wealth sufficient to justify the expense of applying for probate.

By far the most numerous were the stonemasons, with at least ten active in the town at any time. The occupation commonly descended from fathers to sons, and daughters also married masons. The traditional stonemason's skills were learned in the family or close to home: unlike other trades and crafts, the town's masons rarely arranged distant apprenticeships for their sons, and Chipping Norton was the only Oxfordshire town not to send any apprentices to the Masons' Company in London.[16] Limestone for building was readily available from the higher ground east of the town and some masons owned quarries, such as 'Paty's Quarrs' near the Banbury road held by the Paty family. In 1720 a contract for the opening of a new quarry was drawn up between the masons John White and William Meades and the inhabitants of Over Norton, 'to dig stones for the space of twenty years'. White and Meades were required to pay £12 a year and to supply stone to Over Norton at two pence a load. Enterprising masons took up property development and purchased houses for refurbishment and re-sale. At nos 10-11 Market Street, the mason Thomas Taylor owned a large house, probably fifteenth-century in origin like others in the street. In 1695 he built a dividing wall and sold the southern two bays (no. 10) while retaining the northern end (no. 11).[17]

Skilled carpenters were needed both for the renovation of older dwellings and the construction of new ones. The recent survey of Chipping Norton's early buildings has found many roofs of this period added to older houses, such as the rear range of no. 7 Horsefair (now Thai Shire). Both oak and elm were used and there was much re-use of timbers. Slatters were resident in the town but there were no thatchers, probably because most roofs were covered with stone slates, while thatch was reserved for smaller buildings where appearance was less significant and an unskilled labourer could construct a serviceable roof. Glaziers were highly regarded, and several of Chipping Norton's leading tradesmen apprenticed their sons to plumbers and glaziers in Oxford. The Malins family at no. 7 West Street were in business by the 1720s and became well-known plumbers and glaziers throughout the local area for over a century.

Chipping Norton was undergoing more renovation, rebuilding and new construction than at any time since the fifteenth century. Some of it was small-scale, such as the 'little house which I lately built between the stable and the pig-sty adjacent to my dwelling house' of Samuel Higgins in 1737. Other projects saw older houses and cottages replaced, and new buildings on sites hitherto unoccupied. Two new places of worship for dissenters were constructed in New Street, an area where buildings were gradually replacing closes: in 1696 a Quaker meeting house (replaced in 1804 and now a private house) was built at the bottom of the hill, while the Presbyterian (later Baptist) congregation built a chapel in 1733 on a site behind the present Baptist church. The row of houses at the top of New Street on the south side appears to have been rebuilt in the late seventeenth century and no. 8 displays a datestone of 1687. The rebuilding of nos 10 and 10A Middle Row illustrates the continued use of traditional styles and methods. The

37 Nos 4-8 New Street.

38 Nos 10 and 10A Middle Row.

stonemason John Paty left a 'new erected' tenement (no. 10) with an ashlar facade at his death in 1718, and two years later his son applied for permission to extend no. 10A to match it. The facade which now covered both tenements had stone mullioned windows and a continuous drip mould, similar to that on the eighty-year-old almshouses in Church Street, and a timber-framed jettied extension was constructed at the back of no. 10A which would not have looked out of place a century earlier.[18]

Probate inventories for the period 1661 to 1740 suggest the beginnings of a change in living arrangements, reflected in the naming and use of rooms. Ground-floor rooms might now be described as the 'common dwelling room' although most houses still had a room called a hall and some had a parlour. Half of the halls were still used for cooking, in the traditional way, but after 1700 more of the inventoried houses had kitchens and these gradually became the preferred room for cooking. Some kitchens were now integrated into the house-plan with a chamber above them. Upstairs, more chambers had fireplaces, and almost all beds were now on the upper stories. The majority of the dwellings shown in inventories must have been older houses but their rooms could be used in new ways, and the changes evident at Chipping Norton were typical of early eighteenth-century provincial society. The house on the lower side of the market place owned by Philip Wisdom, an upholsterer, for example, had a well-equipped kitchen at his death in 1709, and this was where meals were cooked and dishes were kept. The hall had become a comfortable heated dining-room with two tables and six leather chairs, brass candlesticks, a screen and a looking-glass. The parlour was the sitting-room, with another fireplace, a clock, folding table and chairs, and a desk. Upstairs there were chambers over the hall and parlour and two little chambers over the shop, and a garret in the roof. The chamber above the parlour was the best bedroom and its bed had a feather mattress; this room had a fireplace and a looking-glass, and was furnished with cane chairs and a chest of drawers.[19]

Many of Chipping Norton's inhabitants lived far less comfortably. A house like that of Robert Hawkins, a carpenter who died in 1672, may still have had an open or partially ceiled hall. His house consisted simply of a hall and a chamber, and Robert and his wife must have cooked, eaten and spent their waking hours in the hall. Landlords divided larger houses to provide small units for rent, such as the single property in West Street converted into four tenements by 1672. On the lower side of Middle Row, new buildings were filling the space between the Row and Market Street, and a will of 1722 describes accommodation there among stables, pigsties and a wheelwright's workshop, with shared access to a kitchen hearth and a common pump. This area acquired the nickname 'the College', a name also used at Burford for crowded housing behind tenements. The demand for housing suggests that the town was growing. Population in 1676 was estimated at just over 1,000 and increased in the first half of the eighteenth century. The highway from Worcester and Wales brought a stream of travellers to Chipping Norton, including the travelling poor, and a prosperous market town was an attractive destination for anyone looking for work.[20]

REFRONTING AND THE PURSUIT OF FASHION

While much of the new building was in the local vernacular tradition, some of Chipping Norton's property-owners were adopting new fashions in architecture that transformed towns all over England in the early eighteenth

39 From right to left: Nos 5-9 High Street, examples of early eighteenth-century baroque facades. (Photograph: P.S. Spokes)

century. The process was gradual and piecemeal, largely confined to the homes and businesses of the affluent, and in smaller towns only a few substantial houses adopted the new classical style. Chipping Norton is unusual among Oxfordshire market towns in having a whole street of continuous classical and baroque facades on the upper side of its market place, and many of these houses acquired their new look before 1750.[21] More information about individual buildings can be found in the chapters describing walks around the town.

The classical facade was flat, well proportioned and symmetrical. Old-fashioned gables were no longer desirable and a new house would have a roof with dormer windows, sometimes partially concealed behind a parapet. Sash windows were preferred to the old outward-opening casement windows. Smooth ashlar blocks of limestone replaced traditional rubblestone in the facades of most fashionable houses, although rubble was still widely used for side and rear walls and much is still visible at Chipping Norton today. Brick, however, which became synonymous with the new style elsewhere, was rarely used in the town in the eighteenth century, as stone was close at hand and could be obtained more cheaply. An example of the new architecture, dated by dendrochronology to the late 1720s, can be seen at no. 9 West Street which probably incorporated no. 11 as well; twenty years later the house belonged to a well-to-do baker, Samuel West, who may have been responsible for its construction replacing an older house.

Meanwhile north-west Oxfordshire's aristocratic landowners were building on a much grander scale. The largest project was Blenheim Palace, built for the Duke of Marlborough from 1705. Stone was transported to Woodstock from quarries for miles around, though not apparently from Chipping Norton where either the stone or the quarry-owners were unable to meet Blenheim's requirements. Hundreds of labourers, masons and other craftsmen were recruited to work on the palace. Closer to Chipping Norton, the Duke of Shrewsbury bought the estate at Heythrop and in 1707 began construction of Heythrop House. In the 1720s the Earl of Litchfield built Ditchley Park near Charlbury, and a new house at Bruern for the Copes was under construction. All of these large projects, in addition to numerous smaller gentry houses, rectories and farmhouses built or remodelled in the late seventeenth and early eighteenth centuries, must have greatly increased the demand for labour in the area, especially the services of masons and carpenters. A country house required extensive outbuildings, drainage systems, garden and estate walls whose construction would provide a great deal of

40 Nos 9-11 West Street, built in the 1720s.

local employment. Two Chipping Norton masons, John Clift and William Meades, were paid in 1738 for building a pigeon house at Ditchley Park, and there would have been many such opportunities. The late Stuart and early Georgian spate of construction in the local area must have contributed both to the increased numbers of building workers at Chipping Norton and to the town's economy.[22]

Blenheim and the new country houses also influenced the appearance of the more ambitious new building-fronts at Chipping Norton. Their baroque style was a variation on classical architecture, using projecting bays, prominent keystones above the windows, and ornament on the facade to create a dramatic effect. Among the earliest buildings to be refronted were the inns, which had a commercial incentive to keep up with fashion. In 1720 the innkeeper of the Talbot, John Crutch, was given permission to build his front wall 18in further forward. The building has been replaced but a nineteenth-century painting in Chipping Norton Museum shows an impressive seven-window facade with projecting bays and moulded stone architraves framing the windows. The former White Hart at no. 16 High Street displays the date 1725 on a rainwater head, probably the year in which it was given a baroque facade recorded in old photographs. At no. 2 West Street a handsome early eighteenth-century doorway survives from the Swan, while at no. 23 High Street the Crown & Cushion was rebuilt in 1754 and its facade was brought forward in line with houses already refronted on either side.[23]

Private owners who could afford to rebuild their properties, or at least add a new facade, followed the example of the inns. At no. 1 Market Place a new facade in baroque style was constructed in front of two bays of the older house that survives behind it. One of the most distinguished baroque buildings is no. 7 High Street, which also has a fine early eighteenth-century interior. At no. 24 High Street, Thomas Taylor the ropemaker chose a different style. His neighbour to the north, Hannah Ward, had built 'part of her new additional building … by ranging her new front wall farther upon the common street than the old house stood before'. Taylor moved his front wall forward and converted two tenements to one large house, giving it a smart facade of squared rubble with stone quoins rather than ashlar across both tenements, with projecting keyblocks above the first-floor windows and a stone Gibbs door-surround from a pattern-book published in 1728. The date 1730 on the rainwater heads probably records the completion date of the work. When Taylor died in 1755 his will instructed that the house was to be divided into two separate tenements again for his widow and his son.[24]

41 Rebuilding of no. 10 High Street after a fire in 1967. The scars on the gable wall of the adjoining building show that no. 10 was on a much smaller scale than its grand neighbours and it was probably an older house refronted in the fashionable early Georgian style. (Photograph: P.S. Spokes)

42 Nos 24-25 High Street, refronted as one house c. 1730.

It is unlikely that masons trained in the town would have been familiar with the elements of the new style. Pattern-books were available with guidance on details and proportions, but some expertise was required and it would be interesting to know who designed Chipping Norton's baroque facades. A number of architects and mason-builders active in the local area have been suggested including Francis Smith of Warwick and his son William, the Strong family of London and Taynton, or the Woodward family of Chipping Campden, but no evidence of their involvement has yet come to light.

While nos 24–25 High Street is a two-storey building, many of the houses along the upper side of the market place were rebuilt with three full storeys and attics in the early eighteenth century or soon after. The contrast between their higher roof-lines and the few remaining older gabled houses can be seen in both eighteenth- and nineteenth-century images (Figs 1 and 8). The rebuilding of these valuable commercial properties has also replaced much of their earlier fabric, and along High Street little now remains of the medieval houses which once looked down over the town. There is more to be found elsewhere in the town, as the next chapters will show.

The first part of this book has surveyed the first 700 years of Chipping Norton's history and the clues to be found in its buildings, its streets and in documents that help us to understand its past. Much had changed since the town was established, but the pace of change was about to accelerate. In 1750 the built-up area was still largely confined within the medieval town-plan. Development had begun to spread further out along West Street and down New Street, but the town had been laid out on such a generous scale that most early eighteenth-century construction was infill. Soon after 1750 buildings began to appear above Albion Street, up Rock Hill and along the London Road as the town began its modern expansion. By 1801 Chipping Norton's population had reached 1,800 and a new phase in its history had begun.

In the next chapters you can walk along each of the medieval streets in turn, to see what remains today of its early fabric.

Notes to Chapter 3

1 D. Eddershaw, *The Civil War in Oxfordshire* (1995), 82, 108-10, 164; OHC, BOR1/2/1D/2; CNM, summary of deeds for British School, New Street; TNA, E179/255/3.

2 The leases are with Chipping Norton's borough records at the Oxfordshire History Centre, with copies at the Chipping Norton Museum.

3 M.A. Havinden, 'Agricultural progress in open-field Oxfordshire', *Agricultural History Review* (1961), 73-6; OHC, MS Wills Oxon 67/3/23 (inventory of Simon Trout 1702).

4 OHC, MS Wills Oxon 66/4/10 (inventory of William Thomas 1674); CNM, summary of deeds for 65 New Street.

5 CNM, summary of deeds for 10 Horsefair; London Metropolitan Archives, City of London Sessions: Justices' Working Documents, 10 Feb. 1719-10 Dec. 1720 (www.londonlives.org, version 1.1).

6 OHC, MS Wills Oxon 19/1/12 (inventory of Richard Davis 1698).

7 OHC, MS Wills Oxon 143/1/21 and c.145, f.64 (will and inventory of Nehemiah Norgrove 1693); 143/2/27 (will of John Norgrove 1721); CNM, summary of deeds for 37 West Street; *JOJ* 27 Sept. 1766; TNA, PROB 11/735 (will of John Brayne 1744).

8 OHC, B15/2/45/D/1; TNA, PROB 11/644 (will of John Norgrove 1731); *JOJ* 28 Sept. 1782.

9 OHC, MS Wills Oxon 301/2/31 (inventory of Samuel Blissard 1752); CNM, summary of deeds for 5 Market Place; TNA, PROB 11/696 and PROB 11/941 (wills of Edward Witts 1739 and Broome Witts 1768); *JOJ* 20 Dec. 1800; *Bailey's British Directory* (1784); *Bailey's Western and Midland Directory* (1783).

10 OHC, MS Wills Oxon 143/1/21 (will of Nehemiah Norgrove 1693); CNM, summary of deeds for 5 Market Place; *Daily Post*, 27 Jan. 1731.

11 H.A. Lloyd Jukes (ed.), *Visitation of Bishop Secker, 1738* (ORS 38, 1957), 44, 82; OHC, MS Wills Oxon 73/5/21 (will of John Watson 1720); *London Evening Post*, 3 Aug. 1734, 20 July 1742.

12 J. Ogilby, *Britannia* (1675); R. Blome, *Britannia* (1673), 188; D. Gerhold, *Carriers and Coachmasters: Trade and Travel before the Turnpikes* (2005), 134, 197; *London Gazette*, 6 Aug. 1683; B. Trinder, 'Roads in the 18th and 19th centuries', in Tiller and Darkes (eds), *Historical Atlas of Oxfordshire*, 102-3.

13   OHC, MS Wills Oxon 76/1/31 (inventory of Richard Allen 1675); 171/5/28 (inventory of John Petyfer 1694); 168/4/14 (inventory of John Jaquest 1713).

14   TNA, PROB 11/520 (will of William Taylor 1711); OHC, BOR 1/3/F1/1; *JOJ* 6 Aug. 1768; OHC, B15/2/45D/3.

15   CNM, summary of deeds for British School, New Street; *JOJ* 6 Mar. 1758 and 6 Mar. 1762.

16   Information on apprenticeships can be found in TNA, IR1 (searchable via www.ancestry.co.uk); M. Graham (ed.), *Oxford City Apprentices 1697-1800* (OHS new series 31, 1987); C. Webb, *London Livery Company Apprenticeship Registers*, 27: *Masons' Company 1663-1805* (1999).

17   CNM, summary of deeds for 23 London Road and 10 Market Street; OHC, MS Wills Oxon 73/5/21 (will of John Watson 1720); OHC, PAR 64/10/1D/1.

18   OHC, MS Wills Oxon 134/3/47 (will of Samuel Higgins 1737); CNM, summary of deeds for 9 West Street; OHC, NQ3/1/D4/1; M. Clapinson, *Bishop Fell and Nonconformity* (ORS 52, 1980), 62.

19   OHC, MS Wills Oxon 177/1/32 (inventory of Philip Wisdom 1709).

20   OHC, MS Wills Oxon 81/1/3 (inventory of Robert Hawkins 1672); 23/3/17 (will of Richard French 1679); 114/2/4 (will of Richard Arnold 1722); OHC, BOR 1/3/F1/6-7; Catchpole, Clark and Peberdy, *Burford*, 132, 183; A. Whiteman (ed.), *The Compton Census of 1676* (1986), 422.

21   These changes to the English urban landscape are discussed in detail in P. Borsay, *The English Urban Renaissance: Culture and Society in the Provincial Town, 1660-1770* (1989).

22   D.B. Green, *Blenheim Palace* (1951), 56-9, 237; M. Mobus, 'The Burford school of masons', *Oxoniensia*, 78 (2013), 99-114; A. Gomme, 'Architects and craftsmen at Ditchley', *Architectural History*, 32 (1989), 92.

23   OHC, BOR 1/5/A1/1, ff. 6, 137.

24   OHC, BOR 1/5/A1/1, f.57; MS Wills Oxon 213.213 (will of Thomas Taylor 1755).

A Town Trail

PART II

This section of the book is set out as walks around the historic streets of Chipping Norton. They may be undertaken in any order or separately if so wished.

43 Extract of 1840 map showing High Street and the back lane (Albion Street).

44 Walk map with present numbering.

HIGH STREET

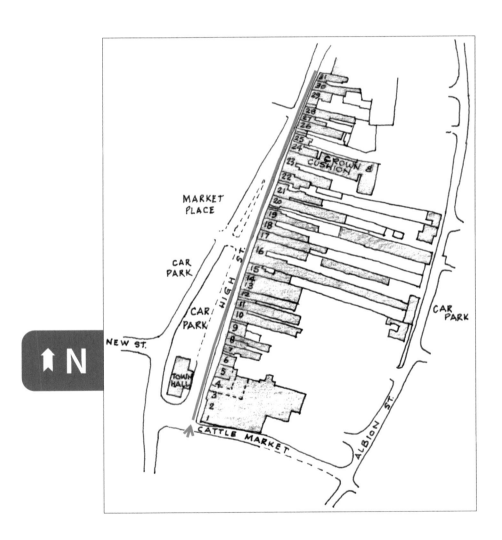

High Street

Hᴵɢʜ Sᴛʀᴇᴇᴛ, which has been known by other names such as Upper or Top Row and occasionally Sheep Street, is nowadays locally called Topside. This name reflects its position on the higher eastern side of the market place; the full glory of the long row of buildings is much admired by visitors passing through the town centre. The present A361/A44 crosses diagonally from the northern entrance to the market place at Horsefair to the southern exits at New Street and West Street.

The setting out of the burgage plots on which these properties were built has been discussed in Chapter 1. Generally the width of these plots along High Street is one and a half perches (a perch equals 16½ft or just over 5m). Although the buildings seen here today are not those that were originally built, there are a few surviving clues to what might have stood here. The usual plan form for these types of buildings fronting a market place include a shop and cellar underneath with side passage leading to the rear yard. Usually a hall was situated behind the shop with a rear wing housing the various outbuildings.

Many trades have been practised along this street over the centuries, not least that of the innholder. In the 1662 hearth tax returns, the majority of the properties here were taxed on between three and five hearths, but the larger inns had considerably more. It is remarkable that so many inns could have found custom in one row as well as all the others in town; sadly only one survives on High Street today. The eighteenth-century illustration of the market place in Fig.1 is a view looking north. Note all the inn signs along the right-hand side, the several houses which still retain their lower rooflines, the old market house in the centre and the narrow entrance to New Street

45 Market Place looking north *c*.1800, with High Street on the right-hand side.

between the buildings to the left of the elm tree. The roof of the former market house was altered in the late eighteenth century by replacing the steeply pitched hipped roof with a flat leaded roof.

The documentary evidence gives a flavour of life in High Street. In the sixteenth and seventeenth centuries there were shoemakers and saddlers connected to the leather industry building up in the town. There was also the usual mix of general trades such as mercers, drapers, butchers, grocers, ironmongers etc., which catered for the everyday needs of the population, and there were barbers who also carried out minor surgery and dentistry, sometimes known as chirurgeons or barber surgeons.

The walk along High Street begins at the south-east corner where one of the most significant changes took place in 1893. The road now called **Cattle Market** was established after the demolition of the property at the south-east corner of High Street and Market Place. This stone building occupied a burgage plot of one and a half perches wide, similar to the rest of the properties in High Street. It had two gables on its street facade with a two-storey canted bay to the northern end, shown in Fig.8. There are similar stone bays on **No.4 New Street** (now Barfield's opticians) which can be compared when continuing your walk in that area (see chapter on New Street). This building would have enclosed the market place leaving only two exits at this southern end: New Street and West Street.

The majority of the buildings now seen in High Street were given extensive facelifts in the early eighteenth century, which sadly means there are no surviving medieval facades. However, the commanding presence of a row of elegant Georgian buildings is very pleasing even with the disparate ground-floor shopfronts. There is documentary evidence of a series of encroachments in front of the former building-line around the 1720s. At this time many house owners applied for permission from the Corporation to add a new front wall to their buildings and this entailed paying extra rent according to the amount of space required.

Another lucrative way of obtaining income for the lord of the manor was by renting out space in the street for sheep pens or stalls on market days. Chipping Norton Corporation, who had acquired this status in 1668, produced leases for the land in front of all the burgage plots on High Street and Middle Row. Most houseowners took advantage of this and the leases survive for many properties, which take the evidence for those particular buildings back to the seventeenth century.

Nos 1-7 are now all in the ownership of the Midland Counties Co-operative Society. Their predecessor, the Chipping Norton Co-operative

46 Pre-1890 view of High Street showing the former building on Nos 3-4 with recessed central section behind a balcony.

47 Drawing of Nos 2-6 High Street, from right-hand side.

Society, was responsible for demolishing and rebuilding **Nos 3 and 4** in 1890. Look up at the central gable and see the datestone. This Victorian building replaced an impressive property with a symmetrical front incorporating a recessed central portion and seven-window arrangement which can be seen in Fig.46 alongside its neighbours, all displaying their Georgian facades. The Talbot Inn was situated here from at least the end of the sixteenth century until 1817 and was used by the Corporation for some of its meetings. Richard Dance, who died in 1668, was probably the innholder of the Talbot; he is recorded as paying for eleven hearths in 1662. Richard's maternal grandfather Thomas Rainsford is also assumed to have kept the Talbot, and his surviving inventory of 1615 lists nine chambers together with the hall, kitchen and brewhouse. John Crutch was the innholder from the 1690s and in 1720 he applied for permission to build in front of this property on a strip of land 1ft 6in by 10ft; evidence of encroachment. John's son Thomas Crutch succeeded him in 1725, on whose death in 1764 the premises were bequeathed to his sister Elizabeth Blissard; she remained the licensee until 1782.

Unfortunately there are very few features left in this row of buildings that relate to the former properties on these sites. **No.5** retains some timbers in the southern wall of the rear wing that may indicate the presence of

48 Jowl post on first floor at rear of No.5 High Street.

timber-framing; a jowl post, with flared ends at top and bottom to support a wallplate and a tie beam, is likely to be earlier than seventeenth century. Fig.46 shows an arched opening in No. 5, to the left of the projecting bay of No. 4, giving access to the rear yard; a similar arrangement to many of the properties along High Street.

Standing in front of **No.7** one cannot fail to appreciate its fine architectural facade: one of the finest in the town and dated to *c.*1720. There were masons living and working in Chipping Norton at this period, and although they may have worked on these grander houses, they may not have been responsible for the design of them. In a History Society talk given some years ago, Tim Mowl suggested that this house could have been the work of Edward and Thomas Strong, leading builders at the time of Sir Christopher Wren, Vanbrugh and Hawksmoor. The Strong family were part-owners of quarries at Taynton and Barrington which produced stone

94

49 No. 7 High Street.

50 Stucco overmantel in first-floor room of No.7 High Street.

51 Dentil cornice in first-floor room of No.7 High Street.

52 Shell cornice in first-floor room of No.7 High Street.

53 Drawing of Nos 11-15 High Street from right-hand side.

for Blenheim Palace. It is not difficult to see some similarities in the distinctive architectural features used here. It is worth taking time to study the use
of various elements such as the fluted Doric pilasters supporting a frieze
of triglyphs and metopes below the plain parapet. Note also the heavy
rusticated stonework used on the ground-floor storey to suggest weight.
Internal features, entirely contemporary with the exterior, comprise dentil
cornices, niches in bolection panelling, a stucco overmantel and doors with
raised fielded panels.

Nos 13 and 14 were formerly two tenements, with No.13 in the hands of
the Quaker Simms family for many years; they were watch and clockmakers
in the town. From the early eighteenth century to 1820 the Black Boy Inn
was situated behind **No.14** with a yard full of hovels stretching up to Back
Lane (Albion Street).

Another elaborate facade can be seen on **No.15 High Street**, now
Barclays Bank. A former townhouse, it was refaced around 1780 in the
Adam-style but the ground floor was remodelled in the 1960s in neo-Geor-
gian style. Note the Venetian tripartite window on the first floor with Ionic
capitals and fluted abaci with flanking blind niches.

The property at **No.16** was the former White Hart Inn and this building
can be traced back to the end of the sixteenth century, but likely to have
been an inn from the fifteenth century, sadly closing in 2003. Now occupying a wide plot of approximately three and a half perches (17m) on High

54 White Hart Hotel and Barclays Bank (Nos 15,16 High Street), *c.*1950.

55 No.16 High Street (the former White Hart) after conversion.

Street, this may have been the result of the incorporation of more than one tenement at some previous time. It is possible to build an impressive picture of the inn, particularly during the seventeenth century. William Diston, who had inherited this inn from his uncle Henry Cornish in 1649, was recorded as having fourteen hearths at the time of the hearth tax in 1662, illustrating the extent of heated rooms in this building. Two stone fire-surrounds survive on the ground floor and one on the first floor, probably dating from the seventeenth century.

Surviving probate inventories list the rooms and their contents, which demonstrate the size of the inn and its furnishings in the seventeenth century. Room names include Worcester Chamber, Hereford Chamber and Cheshire Chamber, reflecting the places to which coaches were travelling. In 1633 the inn had ten chambers, eight heated, including twenty beds, with the inventory total for Richard Coleman of £387 10s 10d. The inventory for Richard Allen, the innholder who died in 1675, had a total value of £458 13s. This included twenty-four beds in fourteen of the seventeen rooms, with evidence of fourteen hearths; this concurs with those listed in the hearth tax of 1662 when William Diston was the owner. The value is reflected in the vast amount of furniture and furnishings within the rooms; the best chamber had a decorative scheme of red carpets, bed curtains and chair coverings amongst other items. This room may have occupied the two central bays on the first floor of the main range, being the principal room in the inn, with the two adjacent rooms on north and south being of a similar quality. Prior to the conversion to residential use between 2003 and 2005 a detailed study was undertaken by Oxford Archaeology. Discoveries included fragments of wall paintings found under later panelling in the first-floor southern room. The pattern of large stylised flowers was similar to embroidery from the sixteenth to eighteenth centuries. The northern room on this floor has square panelling on all four walls thought to date from the seventeenth century with an area of a different design on the east wall probably reset from elsewhere.

This building was given a new facade in 1725; the date can be seen on the rainwater hopperheads if you look up to the eaves line in the central portion. The original arched entrance that gave access to the courtyard and stables for the horses was reinstated in 2005, after being blocked in the 1930s. Take a look through the gates and you will see the whole length of the burgage plot rising up approximately 10m to the back lane at the rear. All the buildings lining the boundary walls were originally ancillary

56 View through archway of No.16 High Street showing jettied first floor on the left-hand side.

outbuildings for the inn; stables, ostler's (person who looks after horses at an inn) quarters, barns, cart sheds, brewhouse and kitchen. There were three known cellars under the property, the most elaborate being under the south end of the front range; investigated by members of the Oxfordshire Buildings Record in 2003. Their report was deposited in the Oxfordshire History Centre (Ref. OBR7) and includes many more details than are mentioned here. The south cellar is very different in character to the north cellar, being an elegant ashlar four-bay stone-vaulted space dating from the seventeenth or eighteenth century that may have been used as a wine tavern. There are blocked window and door openings in the west wall giving access up to High Street. A candle recess exists at the south end of the rear wall and stone steps rise up to the ground floor formerly landing near to the rear of the eastern wall. The previously mentioned inventory of 1675 lists the following items in the cellar: 'a sacke in a pipe' (dry white Spanish wine in a large barrel of 126 gallons) worth £10, 'a runlet (cask) of sacke' worth £6, and runlets of brandy, French wine and sherry worth £3 5s. There was also a separate beer cellar containing seven hogsheads of ale (casks holding forty-eight gallons).

Some other examples of early fabric were uncovered during the Oxford Archaeology recording of 2003. On the rear wall (now internal) of the main range parallel to High Street, timber-framing existed on the first and second floors, which is now encased in modern fabric. This area could have been a multi-storey gallery on the rear of the main range; a typical early eighteenth-century feature which may have been undertaken at the same time as the refronting of the property in 1725. An almost complete late medieval timber-framed gallery 21m long was also found within the northern range running east-west up the boundary of the site. This range retains its external jettied appearance which can be seen as you peer through the present archway, see Fig.56. A first-floor timber-framed wall, supported on timber beams, situated at the back of an open jettied gallery gave access to the lodging rooms behind. These galleries occur in many large inns with a central courtyard. Four areas of archaeological excavation took place in the rear yard at the same time, which revealed small quantities of eleventh-, twelfth- and thirteenth-century pottery sherds. This is consistent with the suggested dating of the layout of the burgage plots.

57 Drawing of Nos 18-21 High Street from right-hand side.

58 Buildings lining the burgage plot behind No.19 High Street.

59 Timber and leaded window in wall between Nos 18 and 19 High Street.

60 Cellar steps and blocked doorway in No.19 High Street.

If you wander up the alleyway between **Nos 19 and 20** High Street, you can imagine how these areas would have appeared in former times. There were many outbuildings lining the boundary walls of this backside area housing cart sheds, barns, grain stores, animal houses, timber stores and other uses. An early window still exists in the southern party wall of the rear range between **Nos 18 and 19** and stone steps formerly leading up from the cellar of No. 19 (see Figs 59, 60).

No. 20 houses one of the oldest identifiable features found so far in Chipping Norton. Under the front range there is a stone-ribbed vaulted undercroft, the ribs rising from corbels with carved heads. One of these heads appears to be an animal, two are probably men and the other is

61 NE corner: carved corbel heads in the undercroft of No.20 High Street.

62 NW corner.

63 SW corner.

64 SE corner.

65 West wall of vaulted undercroft in No. 20 High Street.

thought to be a woman with a headdress dated to 1340–1400. This would give an approximate date of the late fourteenth century for this undercroft, which may have been used as a wine tavern. There are similar examples of taverns in Oxford associated with medieval undercrofts and with direct access to the street, as in this case. Another possible use is as a basement storage area for a shop and hall-house belonging to a merchant of the town, but is possibly too ornate for that use.

There are two stone-traceried windows, *c.* fifteenth century, in the wall parallel to High Street, just below pavement level, and a central doorway giving access to the street via stone steps. The original floor level must have been lower because remains of fifteenth-century mouldings have been found on either side of the door opening at approximately 500mm below the present internal level. Why was the floor raised at some time in the past? It is intriguing to imagine that there could have been other examples of this type of late medieval high-status undercroft along High Street, although none have so far been found.

The Crown & Cushion at **No. 23** is the only inn still surviving on High Street today and has a plot width of two and a half perches. Documentary evidence exists to show that it was the private house of Edmund Hutchins

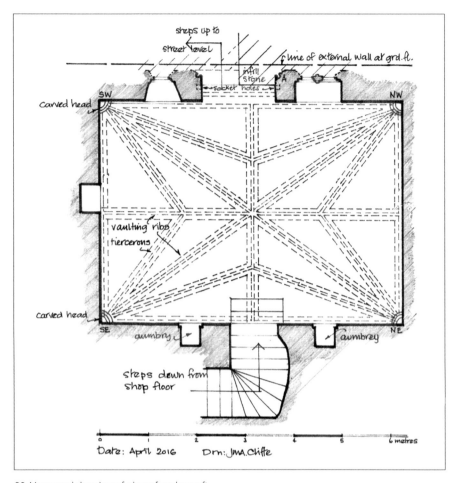

66 Measured drawing of plan of undercroft.

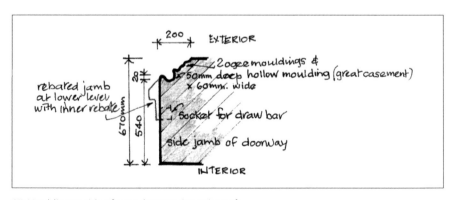

67 Moulding to side of west doorway in undercroft.

68 The Crown & Cushion in the early twentieth century before frontage remodelling.

69 No. 23 High Street, the Crown & Cushion, 2016.

70 Drawing of Nos 24, 25 and 26 High Street.

at the beginning of the seventeenth century. In about 1620 it was opened as an inn by Robert Mayor and called the Crown. By the 1660s the name had been changed to the Katherine Wheel, and later known, at different times, either as the Crown or the Crown & Cushion.

The photograph in Fig.68 shows the eighteenth-century facade on the building before its complete remodelling in the 1930s, giving its present appearance. There have been many other alterations and modernisations in these premises and very little early fabric remains. The cellars were investigated and found to be under the rear part of the front range only; possibly formerly extending through to the street. However, the central archway survives with its cobbled surface leading from the street to the backyard with a few of the many outbuildings that would have stood there. It is good to see this coaching inn still surviving today, when so many have disappeared from the town.

Nos 24 and 25 are now two properties refaced in 1730. Look up and see the date imprinted on the two rainwater hopperheads at eaves level. It is very likely that there were formerly two properties here, each one and a half perches wide, which were converted to one larger dwelling at the beginning of the eighteenth century. There was an inn here in the late seventeenth century kept by Thomas Frayne who died in 1670. These premises were not refronted in ashlar stonework like others in High Street. However, the two-storey facade is a handsome example of provincial Georgian architecture with ashlar quoins and dressings to the row of elegantly arched window openings within coursed squared rubblestone walling.

71 Eighteenth-century doorway to No. 24 High Street.

72 Divided side passage between Nos 25 and 26 High Street.

The archway access at the northern end of **No. 25** leading to the rear is probably connected to its time as an inn. However, the voussoirs of the arch encroach on the neighbouring property to the north; this could be explained by the apparent repositioning of the side wall of No. 26. Look down the passageway and see how it appears to have been widened, possibly to give better access for carriages etc. Note the cantilevered upper floor with timber joists and beams on jowl posts. This passage was later partitioned between **Nos 25 and 26** as it is at present.

The ground-floor ceiling of the present shop in **No. 26** (Oats) has a transverse beam with visible mortices for flat joists indicating a date of possibly fifteenth or sixteenth century, although it may not be in its original position. This beam terminates short of the facade wall suggesting that

73 Stair tower and rear range of No. 26 High Street.

74 Rear gable of No. 27 High Street.

75 Cellar steps in No. 27 High Street.

this building also encroached on to the land in front when being altered in the eighteenth century. Note the straight joints between the quoin stones on neighbouring properties, which show that the refacing was undertaken at different times. This property, along with others, has a roof covering of stone slates laid in diminishing courses; see how this gives the appearance of perspective to the roof surface. There is a stair tower at the junction of the main north-south range and the rear east-west range, visible from the yard. The cellar of **No. 26**, accessed via stone winder stairs, is a small one-bay chamber located to the rear of the north-south range.

No. 27 has a plot width of approximately one perch, narrower than the more southerly properties, but sets the scene for this northern end of High Street, which is far less grand. It also has a much lower ridgeline with an eaves level that has obviously been raised. Look up and note the difference in the stonework just above the first-floor window. The rear range has a steeply pitched roof with central windows on each of the three floors typical of the

76 Narrow entrance from Horsefair showing Nos 28-31 High Street.

seventeenth century. Visible within the present shop (Albion Gallery) there is an existing stone winder staircase (Fig.75) leading down to the one-bay cellar which is inset into a curved recess in the north wall of the property. The cellar is located to the rear of the main range, similar to **No. 25**; this may be a pattern at this northern end of High Street but as many have been filled in and others have not been accessed for this project, it is not possible to be definite. This cellar also has the remains of a stone-mullioned window (now blocked) in the rear east wall. The upper floors are served by a timber winder staircase, still within a curved recess which is probably a surviving feature of the former building. These premises were the site of The Lamb Inn for a brief period in the 1750s, as mentioned in the deeds of the neighbouring premises.

No. 28, is included in the Common Council Minute Book for 1720 when John Payne had to pay 1*s* per annum rent 'for the pales before his windows' (wooden posts to enclose a strip of land to protect the front of the property), because of encroachment on Corporation land. The premises are now known as **Packer House**, see the name on the fanlight above the door. This denotes its connection to the prolific local photographer Frank Packer, whose studio was here from the end of the nineteenth century and whose son Basil continued the business until the 1970s. The town's museum is fortunate to have a large collection of Packer glass plates, some of which are reproduced in this book.

No. 29 was used as an inn, the Blue Anchor, from the end of the eighteenth until the mid-twentieth century. As this occupies a plot width of two perches, it is likely that there were originally two tenements here of one perch each, similar to **Nos 30 and 31**. Another property was attached to the end of this row until its demolition in the 1930s. This area formed the narrow entrance to the market place, which still exists today.

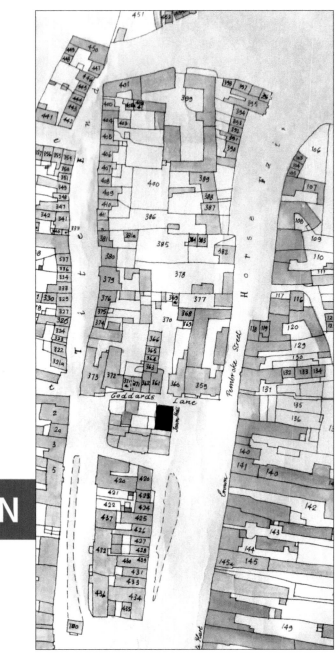

N

▲ **77** Extract of 1840 map showing Horsefair, Goddard's Lane and Middle Row.

➤ **78** Walk map with present numbering.

HORSEFAIR, GODDARD'S LANE AND MIDDLE ROW

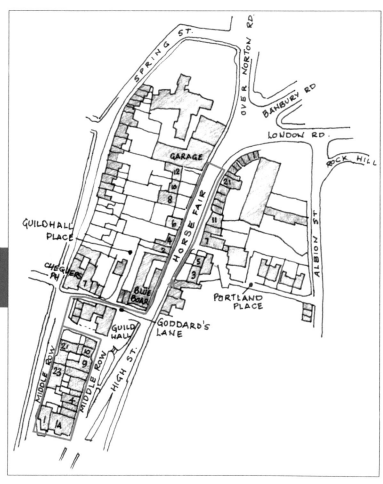

Horsefair, Goddard's Lane and Middle Row

HORSEFAIR

Continuing north from the narrow section of High Street, you enter Horsefair; the widening out of this area was to provide space for the sale of horses on fair days in previous centuries. This northern part of the town was once known as Townsend or Cock's (or Cox) Townsend, a name that survived until well into the twentieth century. Typically for the areas on the edge of the town centre, this seemed to be a poor part of town with bequests noted in wills for the benefit of the poor inhabitants there.

The present barn you can see set back from the road was probably connected to the two cottages formerly attached to the end of High Street (now used as a garage for No. 3 Horsefair). On your right, just past the first two set-back houses, is a small lane, mentioned in deeds as Dark Lane, now leading into Portland Place. In this area was a yard used by blacksmiths, wheelwrights and other tradesmen, surrounded by hovels and small cottages. A 1794 extract from the deeds of premises here mentions that two cottages were built in this vicinity on the site of an 'ancient building' by a slatter (roofer who works with stone slates) called Richard Peregrine Williams; he had bought the land from Joseph Hookham, also a slatter. This information implies that there was a much earlier building in this area.

The building on the northern side of Portland Place, **No. 7**, has a seventeenth-century style to its roof carpentry in the two northern bays. The existing southern bay is thought to have been an infill between a former barn situated across the area which is now the entrance to Portland Place. The present gabled southern wall is likely to be the external end wall of the former barn; note the remains of small triangular openings to provide ventilation for grain storage.

79 Drawing of Nos 7-11 Horsefair.

No. 9 together with several others in the vicinity were owned by Thomas Lord, a mason. In his will of 1768 he bequeathed to his children 'all those three uppermost houses with gardens situated above Dark Lane' and 'all those three lowermost houses and the middle garden.' This description illustrates the complex juxtaposition of buildings and gardens here.

Towards the northern end of Horsefair is a row of buildings with four gables, on one of which is a plaque stating 'J.W. 1870'. These dwellings, known as **Cock's Almshouses**, are now administered by Chipping Norton Welfare Charity and leased to local people. 1891 sales details state 'Opposite front door of Hill Lodge were 4 ancient cottages known as Cock's Row'. In 1824 the Charity Commissioners' report stated that these were '4 small cottages which exist as four almshouses situated in that part of Chipping Norton called Cock's Town's End, for poor people who are placed in by the Corporation, kept in repair by the overseers of the poor, and nothing is known of their origin'. They were demolished and rebuilt in 1870, on the opposite side of the road, in their present position, by John Ward who lived in Hill Lodge (later the War Memorial Hospital). John Ward also requested permission to divert the line of Spring Street in order to give his house a more impressive front entrance and garden; see the two maps at the beginning of this section.

Cross over the road and continue back towards the town centre along the west side of Horsefair past the three houses set back from the road. In 1696

80 Corner elevation of No. 7 Horsefair and entrance to Portland Place.

the deeds of **No. 10** (Eastville) state that Joseph Collett, a carpenter, sold his 'dwelling with a newly-erected house on the south, in Cock's Townsend'. Apparently these premises were 'called by the name of King's Head, lately occupied by Christopher Scott with Thomas Brayne on the south and the garden of George Hasting's house on the north'.

As you walk along the narrow pavement look down the alleyway on your right and notice the cottages and barns set behind the frontages; vestiges of the former backsides (yard or garden) to the original tenements. Pass the side wall of a former barn which is now part of the **Blue Boar Inn** and turn right.

GODDARD'S LANE

The **Blue Boar** started life in the central house of this row of three former tenements. Investigation of the roof structure has established three separate one-bay units divided by thick stone walls, likely to be seventeenth century. In 1668 when the Corporation leased out the sheepgrounds in front of these dwellings, the corner house was occupied by Thomas Somerton, a blacksmith, with the adjacent house in the occupation of Thomas Taylor, a ropemaker, who had bought the house from Robert Berry in 1641. When Thomas Taylor died in 1673 his inventory amounted to a total of £30 3s 4d. His house consisted of five rooms including a shop on the ground floor with three chambers above. There was also a barn over a workhouse with hemp for ropemaking and all his working gear. It was Thomas' son William who must have turned the house into an inn. When he died in 1711 he bequeathed the Blue Boar Inn to trustees for the benefit of his children. There are two cellar chambers, now interconnected, beneath the western end of the property and each of them has a set of stone winder stairs, indicating that they served two separate dwellings at one time. If you have time, step into the bar area and see the stone plaque situated at the side of one of the front windows. The initials stand for William Taylor and 1683 is possibly the date when he established the inn. This establishment has been in use as an inn for over 300 years.

Continue down the lane and you will notice **No. 4**, set back in a yard area. From the deeds it has been established that there was a 'capital messuage' (large house) here with a brewhouse, well, pump and rickyard with access from the street through a passage. Later in the nineteenth century this yard area was called **Guildhall Place** or **Yard** with twelve small cottages

81 The Blue Boar, early twentieth century.

82 Stone plaque for William Taylor.

converted from the old outbuildings. A Victorian historian of Chipping Norton, Charles Kirtland, described the remains of an ancient archway surrounded by later buildings in Guildhall Yard as 'a fragment of a wall three feet in thickness, with pointed doorway, receding bands of moulding, and a small window' which may have been a relic of a large medieval house. Sadly the archway was pulled down and its remains have disappeared.

The two small cottages, **Nos 5 and 6**, on the western side of this yard were rebuilt on the site of one of the King's Hold houses. There were twelve of these cottages scattered around the town, which were bequeathed for the benefit of townspeople by Henry Cornish's will of 1649.

On the corner of Goddard's Lane and Spring Street stands the **Chequers Inn**. There are several early features within this building that provide another example of the late medieval houses found in this particular area of the town (see the chapters on Spring Street and Market Street). Fig.84 shows the extant timber truss in which three of the timbers have been dated to between 1444 and 1476. This truss, with cranked principals (the knees suggesting a possible cruck antecedent), is situated on the second floor above the bar area. With this truss and the other remaining timbers from the original roof construction there is clear evidence that the earliest building here was a narrower tenement with a gable-end fronting Spring Street. Later alterations extended the building southwards with a gable-end facing Market Street; this roof area has been dated to 1613-18. By that time it was a substantial house with its front entrance still in Tite End (Spring Street). In the 1650s it was occupied by Richard Batty, a blacksmith, and it had four hearths in 1662. When he died in 1667 the house became the property of the Norgrove family. Nathan Norgrove, a wealthy tanner, lived here in 1682 before he acquired the tanyard in Church Lane. The house descended to Nathan's granddaughter Mary who married another tanner, Thomas Rouse. After Mary died in 1755 her husband opened the house as an inn called the Blue Anchor.

When the Blue Anchor was put up for sale in 1801 it was described as:

83 South gable of the Chequers seen from rear of Middle Row.

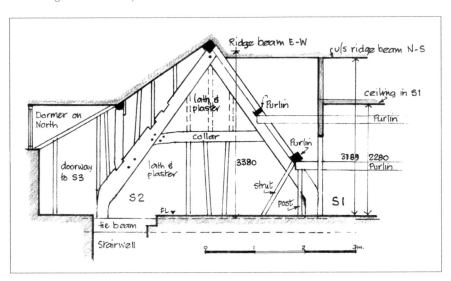

84 Measured drawing of second-floor truss in the Chequers.

that desirable freehold messuage, till lately used as a public house, known by the sign of the Blue Anchor, situated opposite the upper end of Church Street with excellent cellars, good parlour, kitchen, tap room on the ground floor, comfortable lodging rooms on the first floor with garrets over, good brewhouse, scullery, stable, hogsties and other outbuildings with a yard and excellent water.

A ceiling beam in the rear bar has been dated to 1772-1804; this probably dates from the refurbishment undertaken around this time when the name was changed from the Blue Anchor to the Chequers.

Thomas Bucket, the innkeeper from 1827-40, demolished the two old cottages adjoining the inn on the north side and built a stable and coach-house. The Chequers was popular with dealers on market days and advertised 'capital stabling, warm and well fitted up, affording standing room for market and fair days for 50 to 60 horses, spacious lofts, a wide entrance for gigs etc'. The inn was again offered for sale in 1841 when the description of the premises included 'a newly-erected market room on ground floor, 5 good chambers and 5 garrets an underground cellar with pump of never-failing excellent water'. This extract shows how the inn had expanded, incorporating the gable-fronted building on the corner of Goddard's Lane as well as property on its north side giving entrance to the stabling. The premises also had the right of three Commons; proof that it had been three properties each with the right to pasture an animal on the Common. The Chequers was sold to Hall's Brewery in 1867 and is still flourishing today.

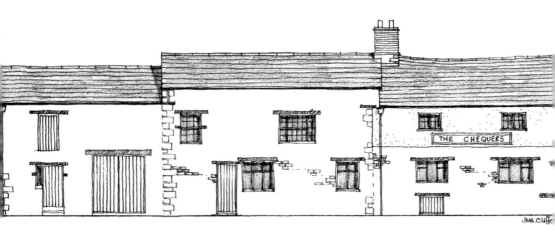

85 Drawing of Spring Street elevation of the Chequers.

Walk round the corner into Spring Street and note the barrel chute into the cellar; this identifies the former front of the building. The cellar is part of the early building that incorporates the fifteenth-century truss. Look at this elevation and note the obvious kink in the external stone wall, showing the point where this property was extended northwards along a different line from the narrow frontage of the original building. The large barn doors, a little further along, were probably the entrance to the former stabling, mentioned above.

MIDDLE ROW

Now proceed back towards the market place southwards along the raised street level at the rear of Middle Row until you reach the corner. This whole collection of buildings, known as Middle Row, is an early encroachment into the large expanse of the original market place laid out in the twelfth century. They may have begun life as temporary structures erected on fair days, which, over time, became more permanent. However, recent research suggests that they may have been deliberately infilled within the market place to achieve a larger number of rentable buildings. They have certainly been a part of the street scene since late medieval times as some fifteenth- and sixteenth-century features have been found in some of the buildings.

No. 1 (now Jaffe & Neale) has a prominent position overlooking Market Place. The survey of the building revealed seventeenth-century features in the southernmost part of the building but with alterations from the eighteenth and nineteenth centuries. There is a barrel-vaulted cellar under the present shop accessed by a partially winding staircase, similar to others in town and almost certainly seventeenth century.

From the western side of the building (rear of Middle Row), look up at the roofline and see the clear distinction between the building fronting Market Place and the attached building at the rear, fronting Market Street. Also note the entrance porch (now disused); this gives a clue to the former grand house that stood here by the beginning of the eighteenth century. Behind this doorway would have been a hallway with a grand staircase (now part of the shop); the stairs survive on the upper floors with the long window lighting the stairwell on the eastern wall. This southern end of the building was formerly a separate dwelling and by the 1750s was in the hands of a mercer, William Bloxham. The second floor contains another clue to the

▲ 86 Drawing of south elevation of Middle Row showing Nos 1, 1A and Bitter & Twisted.

◄ 87 First-floor ceiling decoration in No.1 Middle Row.

alteration of this building. There is seventeenth-century evidence in the timber purlins that the former roof over the southern end was gabled, not hipped as it is now. However, the far northern end of the roof structure clearly has a nineteenth-century construction indicating the various phases that have occurred within this building, now in one ownership.

The rest of this block facing south over Market Place is taken up by the present **Bitter & Twisted** public house on the corner with the entrance to offices in the centre. There were four properties here in the 1750s occupied respectively by William Bloxham, mercer (now Jaffe & Neale), Richard Weston, ironmonger, Francis Bull, ironmonger, and Thomas Guy, tallow chandler, soap boiler and ironmonger in the upper tenement (now Bitter & Twisted). The two gables on the south elevation have been rebuilt several times, and can be compared with Fig.90 where the jetties, which formerly existed on the second tenement from the top, can be seen.

Standing in Market Place and looking at the southern elevation, the wall of the east-west range can be seen at the back of the present first-floor

88 Drawing of west side of No.1 Middle Row.

▲ 89 South end of Middle Row showing two rendered gables.

➤ 90 1948 view of south end of Middle Row showing
jettied gable to No. 1A. (Photograph: P. Spokes)

terrace; note the five-light stone-mullioned windows (Fig.90). The upper
ground-floor room, behind the lower window, houses three beams in the
ceiling, the rear two having mouldings and features indicative of the late
fifteenth or early sixteenth century. Importantly there is another beam in
the first-floor room immediately above, with the same style of mouldings.
These clues indicate that the core of an ancient building lies embedded in
this public house.

A survey of these buildings was undertaken in 1947 and recorded
extremely thick masonry walls around the central gabled building, see
Fig.91. It is known that the town gaol stood in this vicinity and that the
prison or stock house was converted from a butcher's shop *c*.1560, then
rebuilt in 1606 by the lord of the manor, at which time the prison was on
the lowest level with a shop and chamber above. The 1645 will of woollen
draper Henry Fawler bequeathed 'unto my sonne Henry Fawler the shop,

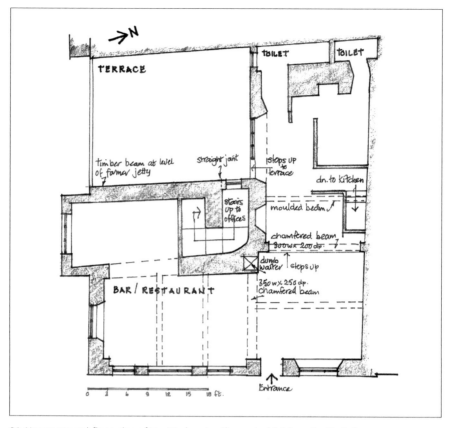

91 Upper ground-floor plan of No. 1A showing the central thick-walled building.

and chamber over the shop, which is over the prison called the dungeon now in the occupation of my son'; this might allude to this building.

In 1874 a deed and plan show the existence of a cellar projecting 17ft into the market place, in front of the central building in this range. Could this denote the frontage line of a row of earlier buildings that have long since disappeared? This has caused much discussion in view of the scant references to a 'Roundabout House' that existed in the market place and was pulled down and rebuilt in 1722. The exact position of this building is not known but Fig.1 tantalisingly shows a large eighteenth-century house protruding into the market place behind the former market house, situated near this top corner of Middle Row. A 1722 lease survives between the bailiffs and burgesses of Chipping Norton and Richard Blagrove, a mercer, for a piece of ground in the market place mentioning 'divers controversies about the alteration and building of a house called the roundabout house lately pulled down and an addition of ground made by enlarging the foundations'. The Corporation granted the lease on condition 'that the building should be built as marked out'. This building was 'adjoining to and bounded northward by the Common Gaol or prison' and contained in length from the prison 29ft southwards and 25ft from the east or upper side to the west or lower side.

The possibility also exists that the gable-end on the corner (Bitter & Twisted) may have been part of the 1722 rebuilding of the former Roundabout House; some early eighteenth-century internal features survive on the first floor of this range (now offices). If this was the case the earlier gabled section may have projected further south and east into the market place and it was this portion that had to be taken down and rebuilt.

No. 3 Middle Row has some interesting internal features that suggest a building of possibly sixteenth or early seventeenth-century date, with some first-floor timber-framing still in situ. The north wall on the first floor, abutting **No. 4**, has rough vertical and horizontal studs set into circular holes at

92 South-east corner of Middle Row.

93 Nos 5-10 Middle Row and the Guildhall.

approximately 300mm centres. This framing sits under a roof truss where the visible principal rafter drops on to a jowl post. Look up above the shop front and note the rendered first-floor wall; this may conceal timber-framing.

Further along in **No. 5**, there is a cellar with another stone winder stair similar to many others in town. There are also square niches set into two of the cellar walls, possibly storage cupboards. From the documentary evidence it appears that this building along with an adjoining one (possibly **No. 6**) was owned in 1668 by Giles Tidmarsh, a cordwainer (shoemaker) and member of a Quaker family. He applied for a lease from the bailiffs and burgesses of Chipping Norton Corporation to set up a sheepground in front of his properties, which at that time were occupied by John Goodwine, currier (leather finisher) and Elizabeth Eldridge, widow. There are similar surviving leases for other properties in Middle Row that give the names of occupants and their occupations.

Continue along this row to **No. 9** (Whistler's Wine Bar) which is a three-bay building housing some early features. If you stop for a coffee notice the finely moulded beams combining cavettos, rolls and cymas indicative of the sixteenth century. There is a substantial stone dividing wall in the cellar which indicates that this may have been two properties with narrow frontages similar to others in this row. The set-back first-floor wall suggests that there may have been timber-framing here as in No. 3.

The next building, **Nos 10 and 10A**, has the appearance of one larger house refaced *c.*1700 in ashlar stone with a continuous moulded string

94 Moulded beam in No.9 Middle Row.

course above the first-floor windows. However, there is a prominent dividing joint down the ashlar skin that suggests that the refacing was undertaken at separate times and reflects the two dwellings which formerly stood here. It is known that there was a fireplace inside **No. 10** of possible sixteenth- or seventeenth-century origin which had been photographed by Frank Packer in the 1900s (see Fig.30); this has not been found. There are ashlar jambs with internal and external chamfers to each side of the entrance door to No. 10. Both properties show evidence in the first-floor window surrounds of former stone mullions and transomes. A large central chamfered spine beam exists in the shop area with ogee stops at both ends and visible wide joists. The first floor also has a chamfered beam similar to the floor below but without any stops.

Note the steep gabled roof on the northern side of **No. 10A** which retains the scars of the roof pitch of the earlier building showing the narrower width. The width of the ashlar face is also clearly seen on this gable showing the amount of encroachment by the later refronting of the earlier house.

95 First-floor jetty on rear of 10A Middle Row.

Walk down the side lane, at one time known as Waring's Lane, named after the Waring family who operated their blacksmith's forge on this corner in the seventeenth century. Looking at the rear of No. 10A you will notice a jettied first floor with light timber-framing of a date possibly contemporary with the front refacing. It is probable that the present rear stone wall dates to the earlier narrow building on this site, and that the jetty was added to the rear to balance the front addition, thus allowing the chimney stack to remain central. Cellars still exist under both these properties, the northern one (No. 10A) having a stone barrel-vaulted ceiling and evidence of a stone-mullioned window in the rear western wall.

The earliest reference to this building appears in the 1649 will of Henry Cornish with his bequest to his kinsman Thomas Diston of Coventry of 'all that house situated in the end of Middle Row where Thomas Waring now dwells' and it is identified as the corner house in his bequest of an annuity from its rents to his nephew Henry Cornish. The Waring family continued here as blacksmiths and in 1689 Richard Waring was granted a sheepground lease 35ft wide outside his property. Richard's inventory, taken after his death in 1698, mentions a buttery, another room, a chamber, garret and his shop containing bellows, anvil, vice and working tools. The 1708 chief rent rolls show that John Paty, a mason, owned this property at that time. His 1718 will mentions that this 'newly erected messuage in Middle Row' has one part occupied by John Eckley and Joseph Bolton and the other part by himself. Being a mason it is likely that John Paty rebuilt these two properties himself some time between 1708 and 1718. Although some of the details suggest an earlier date, a local mason could still have used archaic methods of construction. The evidence suggests that No. 10 was rebuilt first and No. 10A followed shortly afterwards, bringing its frontage forward to line up with its neighbour.

You will notice a small car park area in the lane behind the present Guildhall; this is the site of a former public house that was erected here by John Crawford at some time prior to 1750. In 1752 he mortgaged 'the messuage adjoining Town Hall called the Black Horse' and in 1770 he sold the 'messuage called Black Horse on land where part of the Town hall stood' to William Crawford, a horse dealer. By 1800 this inn had changed its name to the Horse and Groom and later it became a private dwelling known as **No. 19** Middle Row, before being demolished.

There are early nineteenth-century documents relating to **Nos 11, 12 and 13** Middle Row which are described as 'all that messuage formerly the west end of the ancient mansion called the Guildhall and a yard with newly erected buildings'. This could relate to the southern part of the present Guildhall (now the Town Clerk's office), which was added to the original building in the eighteenth century or possibly to another section of building attached to the south-western end.

Now walk round to the front of the Guildhall and you will instantly detect the different styles at either end of the central older section (compare Figs 18 and 96). The southern end was added in the early eighteenth century and the smaller northern section in the nineteenth century. Do look at the fine sixteenth-century stone doorway with four-centred arched head and quatrefoil carvings in the spandrels and chamfered, moulded jambs. This doorway gives entrance to what would probably have been a large open space, but is now a passageway with a large adjacent room on the right-hand side (now WODC One Stop Shop). In the renovations of 2015 plaster was removed from the internal walls that revealed traces of former openings on the eastern side. The opening in the former rear wall, opposite the main entrance, has a wide timber lintel which has been dated to *c*.1520, as have

96 The Guildhall *c*.1900 with Goddard's Lane on the right.

the intersecting chamfered beams set in a grid pattern to be seen in the ground-floor ceiling. Note the daisy wheel apotropaic marks inscribed on the underside to ward off evil (see Figs 99, 100). It is questionable whether or not this space was open on the eastern side similar to other buildings of this type (e.g. the Tolsey in Burford). However, there must have been a staircase up to the first-floor hall within the footprint of the building. The early section of this hall has three bays but a fourth bay may have existed at the southern end before the later alterations. The basis of this suggestion is a document dated 1612 which mentions 'a fair pair of stairs carried up into the said hall from and out of the high street at the east side of the said Capital messuage near the south end, the same to be continued within a convenient Stair case covered and slatted, made and done by the charge of the inhabitants'. This implies that the Corporation intended to make a more convenient access to the upper room than probably existed at that time. If you look up at the left-hand window you will see the shadow of a deeper opening beneath the sill level which could have accommodated a doorway at the top of the proposed external staircase into the first-floor room. Extra evidence for this is the reduced thickness of the wall below this window, only visible internally. If this hypothesis is correct then there must have been an extra bay in this position at that time. The three two-light stone-mullioned windows on the first-floor eastern wall and the three-light window on the rear western wall are all contemporary with the date of 1520.

The first-floor hall, still one large room, was the meeting room for the Guild of the Holy Trinity. After the Guildhall was restored to the townsmen in 1562 the room was used for meetings, then for a town court, quarter sessions and Corporation meetings from 1607 until the new Town Hall was built in 1842. The present vaulted ceiling expresses the shape of the original trusses above; these are not moulded or decorated in any way and therefore were not meant to be visible. The timbers here have also been dated to *c*.1520 coeval with the ground-floor beams and lintel. There are plain stone corbels at the foot of the two trusses across this large room, which seem too large for the slender timbers that are visible below the present boarded ceiling. There may have been more substantial braces at these points attached to the original trusses, but later removed or adapted.

97 Measured drawing of window in the Guildhall.

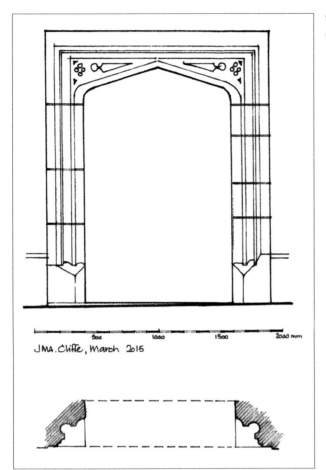

98 Measured drawing of doorway in the Guildhall.

The whole area around the rear of the Guildhall must have been covered by dwellings in the nineteenth century, but have since been demolished, with only the present library and two houses, Nos 17 and 19 facing west, now existing. Continue round to the rear or lower side of Middle Row where there is a walled garden area on the corner of the lane. The first house you come to is **No. 21** attached on its eastern side to a small cottage, now **No. 11** Middle Row. The 1840 map shows this corner area covered by a building that seems to have been part of No. 21 together with the cottage behind it. Some of this building area might have been related to the forge belonging to the Waring family (see No. 10/10A Middle Row).

The first unusual feature seen inside **No. 21** was an arched opening just above ground-floor level in the western wall. Because this area of town is

99 Beams in ground-floor ceiling of the Guildhall.

100 Daisy wheels on a ceiling beam in the Guildhall.

101 First floor chamber in the Guildhall.

102 Nos 21-23 at rear of Middle Row.

known to contain many references to watercourses, this feature may be connected to a possible culvert and be related to an industrial or commercial use of some kind. Late seventeenth-century timbers were found in this dwelling on the ground floor but possibly not in their primary positions, and no cellar was evident. The second-floor roof structure indicated that the eastern side of the building with its steep pitch was typical of the seventeenth century whilst the western side appeared to be eighteenth or nineteenth century. The conclusion appears to be that there was a non-domestic building here which was adapted to a dwelling and parts of it were later demolished to provide a garden area.

No. 22 incorporates a passageway that leads through the double doors to the rear of No. 9 Middle Row; however, the first floor of the dwelling oversails this passage. There are the remains of a large chimney breast on the north wall of the first floor which is also evident in the passage below, clearly belonging to a previous internal layout. The roof construction is visible on the second floor showing the steep pitch and there is another chimney breast on the south wall. This dwelling appears to have been two small cottages of late seventeenth or early eighteenth-century construction.

The adjacent building, **No. 23** (now Kingdom Hall of Jehovah's Witnesses), was an inn called the Parrot from the 1790s. This is a large three-storey building of some prominence occupying a wide frontage on this lower side of Middle Row. Deeds survive to give evidence that in 1695 Elias Andrews, a wheelwright, bought a two-bay tenement from John Durbridge and in 1732 conveyed the same to Richard Weston, ironmonger. In 1777 Stephen Marshall (nephew and heir to Richard Weston) leased 'a stable formerly a house on the lower side of Middle Row with 2 bays formerly occupied by Elias Andrews, now occupied by James Harris'. Then in 1790 the deeds record the release of four messuages in Middle Row, one of which was occupied by Stephen Marshall. It is probable that there were four former buildings here and at least one was used as a stable for a considerable time.

From all the surviving evidence, both documentary and architectural, it would appear that the rear of Middle Row housed non-domestic buildings associated with the premises at the front of the row. Gradually over time, these buildings were converted to dwellings and the other uses that can be seen today.

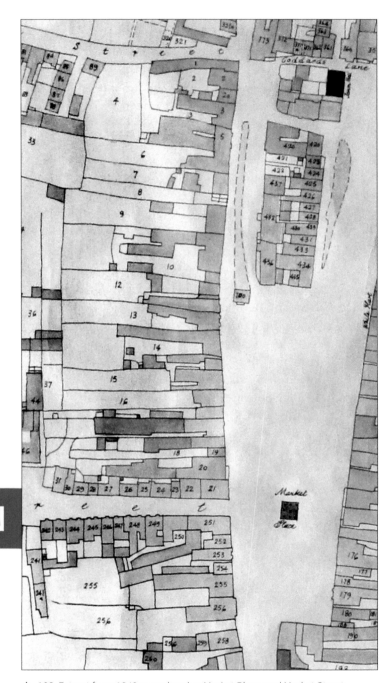

▲ 103 Extract from 1840 map showing Market Place and Market Street.

➤ 104 Walk map with present numbering.

MARKET PLACE AND MARKET STREET

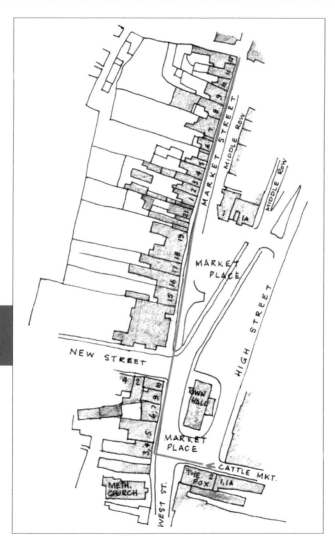

Market Place
and Market Street

MARKET PLACE

Premises on the south and west sides of the market place in Chipping Norton have Market Place as their address. The present numbering begins at the entrance to Cattle Market (a closed corner before demolition of the building on one burgage plot) and continues past the Fox Hotel, across West Street, turning north along the lower side (or nether row), across the top of New Street and as far as the entrance to Market Street. The plots on the lower side are generally wider and shorter than in High Street, around two perches wide (10m) and seventeen perches (87m) long. With reference to the 1840 map it can be seen that a back lane servicing these plots could possibly have extended from Whitehouse Lane (off Church Street) through to New Street just west of the former widening point.

Begin this walk around Market Place by standing near the Town Hall steps, facing south and looking at the facade in front of you. Firstly you will notice the rather grand baroque-style ashlar facade that nowadays is divided into part of the **Fox Hotel** and a flower shop (**No. 1**) with a flat above (**No. 1A**). In 1605 Walter Thomas (the first town clerk of Chipping Norton appointed by the new Corporation in 1607) had bought this house from Anthony Toft, who had inherited it when his father William died in 1585. In the 1662 hearth tax William Thomas was taxed on eight hearths. When William made his will in 1674 he bequeathed 'all my said ancient messuage wherein I now dwell, purchased by my father Walter Thomas gent, from Anthony Toft gent' to his son Henry. The inventory, valued at £385 18*s* and made after William's death, illustrates a grand house with furniture including leather chairs and stools, carpets and cushions, pictures and maps in the parlour. There was a chamber and a garret on the second floor, and

105 Drawing of Nos 1, 1A and 2 Market Place, The Fox.

four chambers on the first floor. The hall was obviously still used for cooking; there were spits, jacks and irons mentioned along with dripping and baking pans. His study contained books and there were four dozen sheets of parchment with his desk and chair in the shop, related to his position as town clerk. There were seven different outhouses in the backside and a cellar under the main range; this has a three-light stone-mullioned window with seventeenth-century ovolo mouldings and iron stanchion bars still in place.

By inspecting the roof structure in Flat **1A** it appears that the eastern end of this range of buildings, all under one roof, was originally a two-bay tenement separated from its neighbour by a thick stone wall. This wall still exists at second-floor level and is positioned slightly to the left of the present doorway to the flower shop. At this point on the ground floor is the beam shown in Fig. 107 with its cavetto and ogee mouldings indicating a fifteenth-century style. Fig. 108 shows the profile of the first-floor beam beneath the truss positioned at the left-hand side of the eastern gable; this has been dated to 1415–47 giving a date comparable with results in Market Street. The present second-floor party wall between Flat 1A and the Fox Hotel is denoted by an existing truss in the wall at the central point of the recessed section. The three bays which indicate the position of the central tenement extend across from the thick wall above the shop door as far as the right-hand side of the western gable, where there is another thick wall encompassing a large chimney stack (seen on the roof) and also a change in internal floor

106 Eighteenth-century doorhead to No.1 Market Place.

levels. This is likely to be the section that was the original Toft/Thomas house mentioned in the documents. At some point in the late seventeenth or early eighteenth century two bays were given a new facade. It would not have been possible to extend across the eastern bay due to the adjoining building at right angles on this corner of Market Place/ High Street (see Fig.8). The remaining part of the range consists of two two-bay sections divided by another stone wall under the central chimney, which were formerly two smaller tenements.

The property at **No. 2** Market Place, now the Fox Hotel, was in the possession of Robert Wirge, a cordwainer (shoemaker), in 1655. It seems likely that there were three properties at the time of the 1662 hearth tax in this section of Market Place and the survey of floor plans confirms this: William Thomas at the top (No. 1/1A), William Barton with one hearth in the middle cottage, Edward Johnson at the lower western end (owned by Robert Wirge) with five hearths. Robert Wirge's will in 1683 bequeathed the house to his wife Elizabeth and also the adjoining cottage, in the occupation of William Barton, butcher. The inventory lists four chambers, hall and cellar with a total value of £14 11s 2d. Robert's grandson Fanshaw Wirge inherited the house and paid a chief rent to the Corporation in 1708 as owner of a burgage property. The actual date when an inn was established is not known, but an advertisement in *Jackson's Oxford Journal* in 1768 stated that John Cleaver was taking over the establishment 'lately known by the Sign of the Chequer, but now changed to the Sign of the Fox': an indication of how inn names moved around the town. Note the large arched opening which was originally the entrance through to the stables at the rear; these were capable of accommodating thirty horses in the sale details of 1845. Take the time to

107 Moulded beam in No.1 Market Place.

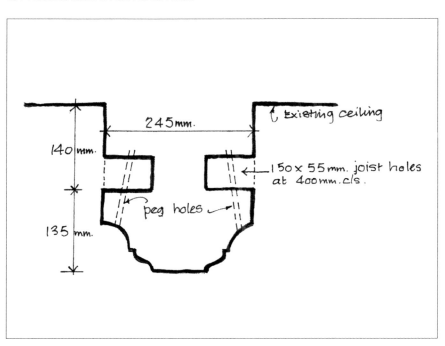

108 Measured drawing of moulded beam in Flat 1A.

109 Drawing of Nos 5-10 Market Place.

stop for a coffee and see the late sixteenth-century stone fireplace in the bar area; this may have been resited here as its size is more suited to a first-floor chamber. You can also walk out into the rear courtyard area to view the long burgage plot extending up to the back lane, now Albion Street. Here you will also see the stone boundary wall of the long range behind the former Swan Inn around the corner at No. 2 West Street.

Crossing over West Street, notice the stone pillar (see Fig.22) standing alongside the Town Hall wall; this is a survival from the former market house. Continue northwards along this lower side to the corner of New Street. In the 1970s, due to the widening of New Street, several properties were demolished on this corner (now Sainsbury's supermarket). After the construction of the widened road, the area left exposed as a building site covered the cellars under **Nos 12-14**; this was the subject of an investigation by R.A. Chambers of the Oxfordshire Archaeological Unit which uncovered remains from several centuries. A 700mm-diameter hearth was let into the floor just inside the remains of the stone wall that fronted Market Place, with a cobbled surface butting up to the exterior. The position of this frontage wall indicated that the late medieval building-line of the market place had not changed up till then. Post-holes and the impression of a sill beam found in the limestone beneath the clay floor suggested there was already a much earlier building standing there. Unfortunately evidence of this former building had been destroyed by the construction of later floors. Some pottery sherds were thought to be fourteenth century but the majority were post-medieval. An iron key and two small pieces of fifteenth- or sixteenth-century glass were uncovered, plus some copper coins from the sixteenth to eighteenth centuries.

No. 14 Market Place, one of those demolished buildings, was known as the Unicorn Inn from at least the early eighteenth century until 1968. However, the building had much earlier origins indicated by the remains of an external sixteenth-century three-light stone-mullioned window still

110 Nos 14-17 Market Place showing the Unicorn in 1947. (Photograph: P. Spokes)

existing in the southern party wall of the present supermarket. This is only visible from the rear yard of **No. 15**, and indicates that a building of some status stood there. The only images that survive of the inn are those taken by Frank Packer in the early twentieth century, with a remodelled facade by that time. The local newspaper in 1790 was advertising cock fighting at this establishment with a sit-down dinner: a flavour of life in the town at that time!

The elegant frontage of **No. 15** was added in the 1780s to convert two seventeenth-century cottages into one dwelling, but features in the rear indicate that an earlier building previously stood here. This house occupies a burgage plot of approximately two perches wide (10m) by seventeen perches long (87m), The three-storey symmetrical facade of this house is

111 No.15 Market Place.

⌃ **112** Remains of a medieval window in rear wall between Nos 14 and 15 Market Place.

➤ **113** Doorway in rear range of No.15 Market Place.

114 Internal view of small window at rear of No. 15 Market Place.

constructed in ashlar stone with a parapet, moulded cornice and corner pilasters. The ground-floor windows are Palladian-style (sometimes called 'Venetian') with Doric columns dividing the three sections, flanking a tall entrance doorway with reeded and banded architraves and projecting flat hood above a fanlight. This is all consistent with the architectural style of *c.*1780 and the interiors of the frontage rooms also include features of this period. The rear ranges of the house still have the feel and style of the former cottages and have some interesting surviving elements hinting at the earlier building on this site. A small single-light window with pointed arch and deep splayed internal aperture exists in the lower ground floor of the rear range, possibly dating from the fifteenth century. Alongside is a doorway having large splayed stone jambs with broach stops and a timber lintel with a carved-out shallow arch, probably fifteenth or sixteenth century. These features, along with the window belonging to the former adjacent building, suggest the existence of late medieval houses along this lower side of the market place.

The next building, **No.16** Market Place, is now a bank but had been rebuilt as a three-storey townhouse at a similar date to its neighbour, *c.*1780. It is highly likely that this house was also converted from two former cottages on the site. Also built of ashlar stone, it has a bracketed cornice over the first-floor windows, a plain parapet and rusticated quoins. The bull's eye window on the second floor is an unusual feature in Chipping Norton. The first-floor windows have eared architraves, keystones and bracketed sills; the central window having a slightly projecting pediment. The ground floor was probably remodelled when converted to bank premises in the late nineteenth century, by including rusticated arches to the four openings. This treatment was also used on the lower floor of the present Town Hall, which you will have noticed as you crossed New Street.

Nos 18 and 19, now also bank premises, stand on the site of two former burgage plots. Fig.118 shows the former street scene with an imposing three-storey house with central projecting porch at No.18 and the adjacent inn, the Borough Arms, at No.19. Although the bank is of a later period than this study is concerned with, it is worth looking inside the banking hall to see the magnificent stained-glass domes in the ceiling. The main reason for including this nineteenth-century building is due to the fact that an exciting discovery was made in the garden to the rear. A Victorian summerhouse is built against the southern boundary wall, which includes two fine arched doorways of late fifteenth-century style. They are constructed

153

▲ 115 Drawing of lower side of Market Place showing Nos 16-19.

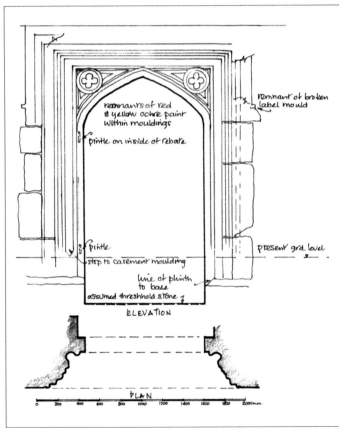

remnant of broken label mould

remnants of red & yellow ochre paint within mouldings

pintle on inside of rebate

pintle

step to casement moulding

present grd. level

line of plinth to base

assumed threshhold stone

ELEVATION

PLAN

0 200 400 600 800 1000 1200 1400 1600 1800 2000mm.

◄ 116 Measured drawing of archway at rear of 18 Market Place.

154

117 Two re-set archways at rear of No.18 Market Place.

118 Nos 14-21 Market Place showing Borough Arms at No.19.

155

of local oolitic limestone and both retain traces of ochre colouring. The high-quality decorated doorway has deeply cut quatrefoils set in spandrels with a roll moulding appearing to be a double cyma, possibly dating to the fifteenth century. The other doorway is very different in design with a Tudor arch and plain cavetto moulded jambs. Both openings are set on to a rubblestone plinth and have clearly been re-set from elsewhere to create this garden structure. They may have come from one of the earlier buildings on this site, possibly the Borough Arms, or another building in this vicinity, in view of the fact that other similar styled arches have been found in this area of town.

This lower side of Market Place consisted of some very fine town houses in the late eighteenth century, all suspected to have been rebuilt from former more modest dwellings. This gentrification was of a slightly different character to the upper side (High Street), which had mostly been undertaken some years earlier, c. 1730.

MARKET STREET

Nowadays Market Street begins as you leave the north-western corner of the market place and continues to the top of Church Street. Formerly this street was considered to be part of the market place and was a continuation of Lower Side or Nether Row, as explained in the Market Place section above. It is likely that the burgage plots here were laid out at the same time as the rest of the lower side of Market Place and possibly before Middle Row was established. This area has proved to be extremely interesting due to the survival of many internal features from the fifteenth century onwards. This has led to the belief that the houses here represent some of the oldest surviving in the town, and may well have been high-status accommodation for townspeople in the late medieval period.

From the dendrochronology testing undertaken on several buildings in this area, it is now known that there is surviving fabric dating from early to mid-fifteenth century that is not visible externally. The architectural nature of these properties is very different from High Street and Market Place: these had not been gentrified during the eighteenth century by adding ashlar facades. It seems that this street may have become a less desirable place to live over time, and the houses were not so radically altered as those nearer to the central market place. Over the centuries

▲ 119 Market Street, c.1900.

▼ 120 Nos 1-5 Market Street showing entrance to Victoria Place.

121 Drawing of Nos 6-9 Market Street.

they appear to have been divided up into smaller dwelling units with some shops on the street frontage.

As you enter this street from Market Place, you are immediately aware of the different nature of the buildings here. The fact that the western side is very much lower than the opposite side (rear of Middle Row) gives a feeling of being in a narrow street of small dwellings. It is obvious to see how the road levels have risen over time when you notice the low-level window sills; most houses having steps down from the front entrance doors.

The first thing you notice on your left, between **No. 22 Market Place** and **No. 1 Market Street** is an archway leading to an area which has been called **Victoria Place** since the 1870s. This is now a quiet secluded backwater containing seven dwellings, some converted from older outbuildings. There were stables, barns and piggeries here at one time and these would have been connected to the trades of the occupants of the frontage properties. Michael Butcher owned three properties here in the mid-1750s, and lived in one of them; Michael was a baker and would have had his bakehouse in this vicinity, maybe in the yard at the rear. He sold one of these dwellings to James Phillips, also a baker, in 1755 who lived here until his death in 1768. James' will assumed that his wife would carry on the bakery business as he left her all the 'uses, profits, rents and all other benefits arising for the purposes of carrying on my trade supporting herself and the children'.

As you pass the butcher's shop at **No. 1**, look inside and notice the steep steps down to the inner floor level which is a common feature in this street. Note also the small pointed arch in the rear wall opposite the entrance door;

this is similar in style to others that have been found in this area of town and possibly dates from the fifteenth century. It is likely that **Nos 1, 2 and 3** may have been one tenement with a yard behind it, the present thin party wall between Nos 2 and 3 suggests a link.

Walk northwards along the street towards **Nos 6, 7, 8 and 9**; these four houses have been extensively surveyed in order to establish how these properties were originally built. The deeds suggest former links may have originated between them in various combinations. Look up and notice how the eaves line is higher over **No. 7** in comparison with **Nos 6 and 8**. Although not refaced in ashlar like the houses in High Street, these cottages have had their frontages rebuilt at some time in the past as indicated by the fenestration. Notice how the wall at first-floor level of **No. 8** is rendered, perhaps concealing former timber-framing; this wall is much thinner than the other stone walls below. Further evidence of this type of construction also exists in the rear wing of this house, which incorporates the remnants of a jettied first floor, as shown in Fig.124.

Surviving deeds from 1609 when Arthur More, a tailor, was living in **No. 7**, include a very complex description of the properties and the partitions between the garden grounds attached to them. It could be at this time that **No. 6** and part of **No. 7** were one dwelling and the house was to be divided between Arthur More having the northern half (part of No. 7) and Edward Dawson, a shepherd, having the southern half (No. 6).

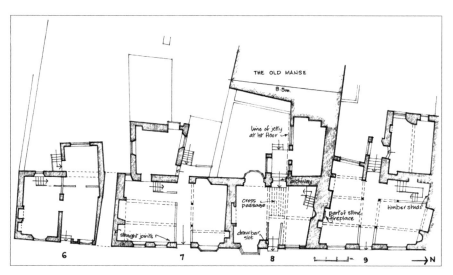

122 Ground-floor plans of Nos 6-9 Market Street.

123 Archway in rear wall of No.8 Market Street showing cross-passage timbers.

124 Rear of stone arch and remains of jettied first floor in No. 8 Market Street.

The deeds for **No. 8** begin in 1618 when it was in the hands of Sir William Cope of Hanwell; his father and uncle, Sir Anthony and Sir Walter Cope, had been involved in purchasing former Church properties from James I. This may have been one of the properties formerly belonging to the chantries of Chipping Norton church which were sold after the dissolution. At this time the house was sold to William Warde, a maltster who lived there until his death in 1632. By 1757 the three properties **Nos 6, 7 and 8** were inherited by Mary Lord.

As illustrated by Fig. 122, the plans appear quite complex and the present boundaries between the properties seem to deviate from possible earlier burgage plots. **Nos 7, 8 and 9** clearly show that they had cross-passages with remaining timbers to substantiate this theory. All four of these houses have internal features that suggest that they are much older than originally thought. **No. 8** has a well-preserved stone arch on the original rear wall similar to **No. 1** Market Street of a likely fifteenth-century date. It is highly probable that the neighbouring houses also had stone arched doorways at one time. This rear archway together with the opposite doorway on to the street would have been at either end of a cross-passage, a typical arrangement in the fifteenth century. Fig.123 shows the wide, flat ceiling joists across this passage with a transverse beam on either side. The slots still survive on the underside of these beams indicating the position of the timber screens separating the rooms on both sides. The front entrance has an interesting feature: a hole 100cm square in the wall to the southern side of the doorway; this is a socket to take a draw bar fitted across the door for security purposes.

The first floor also provides more evidence of this ancient dwelling; a large stone fireplace with ogee mouldings and chamfered edges probably dating from the fifteenth century and consistent with the dating of the timbers. In the same chamber was another exciting discovery: the lower part of a

➤ 125 Drawbar slot at side of front entrance doorway in No. 8 Market Street.

▼ 126 First-floor fireplace in No. 8 Market Street.

➤ **127** Assembly marks on timbers of first-floor truss in No. 8 Market Street.

▼ **128** Lower part of truss visible on first floor of No. 8 Market Street.

▲ **129** Upper part of smoke-blackened truss in roof-space of No. 8 Market Street.

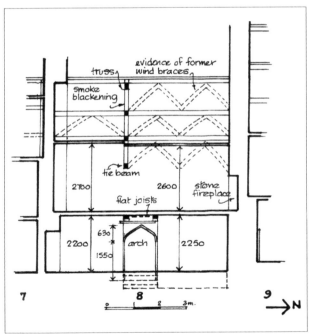

➤ **130** Section through No. 8 Market Street.

163

↟ 131 Remains of a carved and moulded fireplace in No. 9 Market Street.

➤ 132 Measured drawing of jamb moulding of fireplace in No. 9 Market Street.

large truss with clearly marked carpenter's assembly marks. The upper part of this truss is within the roof space and the timbers in this upper area are smoke-blackened on the southern side, indicating that this was originally an open-halled house with a central fireplace, the smoke rising up to the roof area and exiting through louvres on the ridge. Timbers from this truss together with the ground-floor beams have been dated to 1424-56.

The purlins associated with this truss have the remains of wind-brace slots which are shown dotted in Fig.130. The configuration of these suggests that there were three rows on either side of the roof indicating a high-status dwelling. The adjacent bay in **No. 7**, which also has evidence of wind-brace slots, was probably part of this house making it a three-bay dwelling.

At the next house, **No. 9**, look up and notice the Britannia fire insurance plaque below the eaves. Although this house has a very different facade to its neighbours, the internal features appear to be of a similar age. The deeds suggest that this could also have been a former chantry property and was also in the hands of William Warde in 1618, along with **No. 8**. By the 1740s the house frontage had been radically altered and this property had become the Plough Inn held by Thomas Sparrowhawke. As previously mentioned there is also evidence of a cross-passage in this property, and several areas of light timber-framing on the rear walls of the first and second floors. An intriguing relic of a stone-arched opening exists alongside the more modern fireplace in the front room on the ground floor. This could be the remnants of a very high-status fire-surround of a late medieval house. The seemingly low level of this feature can be explained by the knowledge that the ground-floor level of this house has been raised from its original position.

These premises along the lower side of Market Place and Market Street, together with those in Spring Street and Goddard's Lane, include remnants from late-medieval times and have been some of the most exciting discoveries in this study.

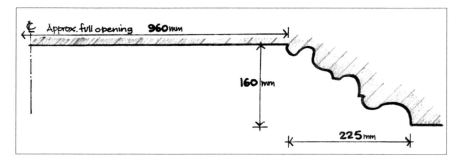

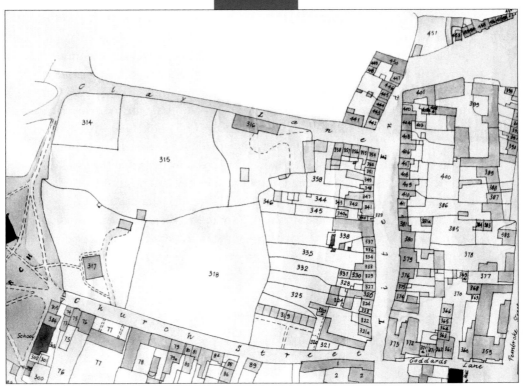

▲ 133 Extract of 1840 map showing Tite End, Clay Lane, Church Street.

➤ 134 Walk map showing present numbering.

SPRING STREET, CHURCH LANE AND CHURCH STREET

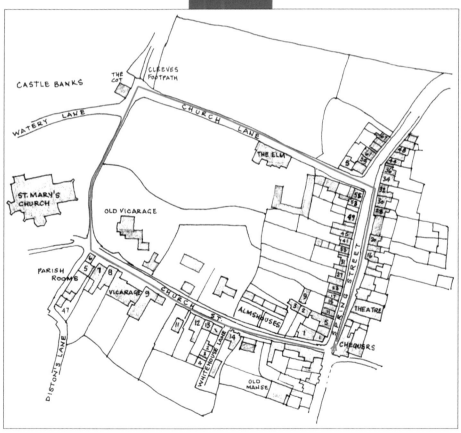

Spring Street, Church Lane and Church Street

SPRING STREET

The former name of **Spring Street** was Tite End until the 1850s or therea-
bouts. A tite is the local word for a water source: a spring, pool, tank or
trough. The tite itself must have been situated somewhere along this street
which lies on the spring-line between the underlying layers of limestone and
clay. The numerous springs that emerged in this area flowed down towards
the Brook behind the Castle Banks. The two different levels of the street
became known as the upper row and nether row of Tite End; this situation
occurs elsewhere in Chipping Norton due to the steep slope down from
east to west.

From at least the end of the sixteenth century the street was an impover-
ished area; charitable bequests in wills left money for 'the poor people living
in the Tite End'. Much of the housing consisted of small cottages, often
tenanted, although there were a few more substantial houses in the street.
From the eighteenth century many of these were sub-divided into smaller
dwellings with alleys and courts behind them, some of which still survive
today. From the sixteenth to the mid-nineteenth century one of the town's
large tanyards was located in Church Lane (formerly Clay Lane) leading off
the north-western end of Tite End. The existence of watercourses would
have been a significant factor in the siting of a tannery here. This led to the
growth of numerous trades related to leather-working in this area such as
shoemakers, glovers and harness-makers. There were also butchers who
had slaughterhouses behind their cottages and would have supplied skins
to the tanners.

135 No.1 Spring Street.

136 Nos1 and 5 Spring Street (incorporating former No.3).

137 Lower section of truss with arched doorway on first floor of No. 1 Spring Street.

138 Upper section of truss showing arched collar on second floor of No. 1 Spring Street.

As you walk from Market Street towards the beginning of Spring Street note the steeply pitched roofline of the building that projects forward of the corner property, formerly No. 3. This is a good indication of surviving early fabric, particularly roof timbers. **No. 1** now incorporates the house on the corner and most of the former **No. 3**, with the adjacent **No. 5** completing the range. The three-bay section under the steep roof has a well-preserved timber-framed wall (only visible in the northern part of **No. 1**) rising through two floor levels, within a truss which has been dated by dendrochronology to the mid 1450s. This truss includes an arched doorway at first-floor level; unfortunately the north side of this doorway is not visible in the adjacent property (**No. 5**), although it may survive beneath the wall covering. A central raised cruck truss survives across the former two-bay open hall and there is evidence of wind-braces in this roof structure. There was probably a gallery leading to a room beyond the doorway. A later inserted floor is indicated by heavy intersecting beams supporting the first floor in the southern bay; these are almost certainly of a later date than the trusses. It would appear that **Nos 1, 3 and 5** were all part of the same tenement with the southernmost section of the present No. 1 on the corner being a later addition.

139 Spring Street looking north c. 1900.

171

JMA.C
© 2014

140 Drawing of Nos 29–33 showing access to Nos 35-39 Spring Street.

This late medieval house was owned by a wealthy widow called Joan Mitton, who died in 1530 and is buried in St Mary's church. Her memorial brass recorded that she had been married three times, to Thomas Kilby, grocer, Thomas Tanner, mercer and lastly to Griffith Mitton, a gentleman who died in 1518. After the death of her third husband Joan bought this house and another one at the top of Church Street to fund prayers for her soul after her death. In 1731 the will of John Berry, a barber chirurgeon, bequeathed this house and the horsepool behind it to his brother. He had acquired this property in 1695 from John Harris, a physician, when it is mentioned as having Church Street on the south and a messuage occupied by John Hutt, a glazier, on the north (**No. 5**). Note the entrance to the alleyway between **Nos 5 and 7** which can also be seen in Fig. 136; one of several along this lower side of Spring Street giving access to other properties at the rear.

Many of the properties on the upper or east side of this street have been rebuilt, but some of the lower side buildings have retained a few clues to their earlier construction. However, alterations over the years mean that some timbers may not always be in their original position, thus making it very difficult to interpret the original structures.

On the lower side, look at the facade of **No. 33** and notice how it differs from its neighbours. Note the use of ashlar in the horizontal band across the top of the door and windows and the side jambs of the doorway. The rendered wall to the first floor of **No. 31** probably masks former timber-framing in this position, whilst No.33 has been much altered in the eighteenth century by raising the roof and refacing the front wall. There is an encroachment on all floors at the rear of No. 31 northwards into No.33. There is no evidence of a truss on the second floor of No. 31 but there is a truss in No.33 approximately 1m to the north of the present party wall, which suggests that subdivision has taken place. From the deeds of **No. 33** this house is known to have been occupied by William Hastings in the 1690s; he had been the town clerk since 1675.

Now cross the street to the upper side and look at **Nos 30-34**. It is possible to discern the former eaves line on **No. 30** if you look carefully at the

141 Ground-floor moulded ceiling beam in No. 30 Spring Street.

142 Ground-floor moulded ceiling beam and joists in No. 32 Spring Street.

143 First-floor timber-framed wall in No. 34 Spring Street.

change in the style of the stonework. Documents of 1745 describe a property here as 'formerly a farmhouse in Tite End with a right of Common'. It has not yet been determined which of these three properties may have been combined to form the farmhouse. There are some early features in all three which are similar in style; moulded timber beams and fireplaces of a possible mid-seventeenth century origin. The ceiling in the ground floor of **No. 32** is exceptionally fine with an ovolo-moulded beam and all joists showing scroll stops, intended to be visible and indicating a high-status room. There is internal and external evidence of wider window openings on the street elevation of **No. 34** with visible remains of timber lintels. Look up at the first-floor windows of **No. 32** and you can see still the remains of stone sills under the existing timber frames. Further evidence of a possible connection between **Nos 30 and 32** is the presence, at the side of a common chimney stack within the present party wall, of a dressed stone jamb of a fireplace opening with a suspicion of an arched head in both properties on the first floor. The assumption remains that **No. 36** and perhaps the northern part of **No. 34** may have been a barn attached to the former farmhouse.

144 Fireplace in No. 30 Spring Street.   145 Fireplace in No. 32 Spring Street.

146 Nos 30-36 Spring Street.

You will realise, by comparing the two maps at the beginning of this chapter, that the north-east end of Spring Street had been realigned at some time after 1840, at the request of John Ward, who lived at Hill Lodge (later the War Memorial Hospital). The last dwelling now on the western side of Spring Street, **No. 67**, was described in 1915 as the last remaining cottage known as King's Hold houses; these were bequeathed to the Corporation by the will of Henry Cornish in 1649.

Walk back towards the corner of Church Lane where there was a property with surviving documents dating back to 1618 described as 'in the nether rowe of the Tyte End'. Henry Cornish conveyed to John Brookes the south part of it, containing four and a half bays which included two lean-to rooms and an entry and also the right to pasture a horse or rother beast (horned cattle) on the Common. Sampson Allen and his son John were occupying that south part of this property and John Tarless lived in the northern part. In 1639 the part on the west of Sampson Allen's house is described as having 'three rooms called the hall, inner chamber and cow house containing four bays'. It is also described as 'already set out and divided from the other part in possession of John Brookes'. There was also land on the western side of this property accessed from Church Lane (then Clay Lane). By 1744, the property was in the hands of a tanner, Thomas Kirby, and then conveyed to Samuel Bowers, another tanner, in 1760. By the early nineteenth century fellmongers (dealers in hides) were in possession and in 1828 premises in this vicinity are described as 'a cottage in Clay Lane, warehouse, skin yard, water pools, lime pits, beam house and garden'. Tanyards are notoriously smelly places and this end of town would not have been a desirable place to live at that time.

CHURCH LANE

This was formerly known as Clay Lane, and leads down from Spring Street westwards towards the Castle Banks. Nowadays there are only a few houses here, but the field on the northern side of this lane has many tell-tale humps and bumps suggesting that there have been some buildings here in former times. The various premises connected to the tanyard known to have been in this area could account for this evidence, alternatively there may have been cottages here from the time of the early town of Norton. This lane was possibly the main route down to the castle for travellers coming from the direction of Oxford. Early thirteenth-century documents held in Brasenose

College archives relate to these lands, which originally belonged to the Priory of Cold Norton. One of these is dated *c*.1260, and mentions the house of Alexander de Rollandrich 'the tenement which is nearest to the gate of the castle, between that inhabited by John son of Geoffrey Black and the house of Teiha daughter of Luke'. There was almost certainly more than one gate to the castle so this deed might not relate to the bottom of Church Lane. However, another document, of 1330, mentions the tenement of John the Apparitor (an official of the church court who summons witnesses to appear) 'in the street which is called Cleistrete'. These deeds give an insight into the names and occupations of people living in this street, but there is no further evidence of the buildings which may have stood here more than 800 years ago.

The large house that now stands on the southern side of Church Lane called **The Elm** has been the residence of several prominent townspeople since the mid-nineteenth century. This building presents a rather gaunt appearance on its north side abutting Church Lane but its principal face is now on the south garden side accessed through the gateway. The original part of the house appears to be early eighteenth century with later nineteenth-century additions on the east, west and south sides, probably undertaken when inhabited by the Rawlinson family. The central three-storey building has a steeply pitched roof of three bays with carpentry features similar to those found elsewhere in the town.

Continue walking down the lane towards the Castle Banks where the lane divides. At this point a footpath known as The Cleeves turns northwards, skirts the eastern edge of the Castle Banks and follows the line of the Brook towards the hamlet of Over Norton. Before the present Over Norton Road was built, this path was the main route between the village and the town of Chipping Norton and at the time of enclosure, in 1770, was stipulated to be retained at 12ft wide. Standing here and looking towards the Castle Banks it is possible to visualise where a gateway to the castle may have been sited – note the dip in the mounds almost opposite the end of the lane. Although no archaeological excavation has been undertaken, some initial surface survey work (unpublished) has been done by students in recent years suggesting the positions of buildings within the bailey areas and the sites of possible gateways. The main entrance might have been on the south-western side of the site due to the fact that the main road from Worcester approaches from that direction. The castle would certainly have appeared an impressive structure from that side, rising high up above the road in the valley.

147 The Elm on the south side of Church Lane.

▼ **148** Castle Banks from bottom of Church Lane.

▲ **149** North side of the Castle Banks, early twentieth century.

179

CHURCHYARD

Now turning left and following the path alongside the stone wall you will pass through the churchyard. It is not intended to embark here on a lengthy description of the impressive architecture of the parish church of **St Mary the Virgin** as this beautiful Grade 1 listed building has been well-documented. However, there are some interesting items which are worthy of inspection on the exterior as you walk by. Down at ground level on the eastern wall of the chancel, notice the thirteenth-century buttress which is considered to be one of the earliest surviving pieces of the church fabric. The adjacent blocked narrow opening with a fourteenth-century pointed arch is connected to the basement area which was probably a former crypt. By the early eighteenth century this was noted to be a charnel house; there are internal remains indicating a vaulted arched ceiling visible below the floor of the former vestry. The doorway on the south side of the chancel features in the 1546 will of Thomas Fryday, a mason. He asked that 'my body to be buried in the churchyard of Chipping Norton before Saint Sunday beneath the chancel door'. Saint Sunday appears in wall paintings

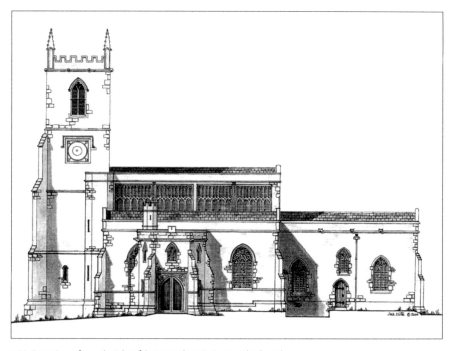

150 Drawing of south side of St Mary the Virgin parish church.

151 Remains of thirteenth-century buttress and fourteenth-century blocked opening.

181

152 South chancel door.

153 Gargoyles on parapet of the south aisle.

in English churches depicted as a figure of Christ surrounded by tools of various trades and was therefore regarded as the working man's saint. It is possible that a representation of St Sunday appeared in the window above this doorway, or was there, perhaps, a statue in a niche placed centrally above the door, which was later widened into a two-light window?

Note the finely carved stone gargoyles on the parapet as you walk round towards the south porch. This is a rare two-storey hexagonal structure and a beautiful example of fourteenth-century architecture, note the ball flower mouldings around the inner south door. Look up at the stone bosses on the vaulted ceiling with a devil, sheep and green man. Continue round the perimeter of the church until you come to the north-west corner of the outer north aisle; look up at the window and see the wool merchant's shields set on either side. They could be the marks of the founder or benefactor of the chantry chapel of St John the Baptist situated inside the east end of the outer north aisle. Compare Figs 156 and 157 where the initials on the shield inside the church appear to be very similar. Do return later and enter the church, pick up a leaflet and take a look at the wealth of treasures inside, there is so much to see.

154 Ceiling of the south porch showing stone ribs and carved bosses.

155 Ball and flower moulding around the south doorway.

156 Shield on interior of the east window of the north aisle showing merchant's mark and initials.

157 Shield on the external wall of the north aisle showing merchant's mark and initials.

158 Drawing showing Nos 6 and 5 Church Street and Parish Centre.

As you walk back across the churchyard towards the bottom of **Church Street** stop and look at the building on the corner, cottage **No. 6** with the adjacent **No. 5**, (formerly a cottage but now the entrance to the church office).

CHURCH STREET

Look at the north-east gable of **No. 6** and note the symmetrical fenestration of three blind windows with a central chimney above; this has been the subject of much discussion. At first glance these windows appear to be sixteenth century in style but on closer inspection it seems more likely that this gable has been rebuilt at some time during the nineteenth century and that the present windows are neo-gothic. However, the three one-light windows on the churchyard elevation appear to be identical with those in the Guildhall, dated 1520. Internal inspection of the roof structure suggest late sixteenth to early seventeenth century supported by the style of timber preparation, joinery and assembly marks. On the south wall, adjacent to **No. 5**, within the roof space, there is evidence of a lower gable of steep pitch similar to the present roof, and a change in masonry and surface finish. This suggests that this wall, which is now a party wall between **No. 6 and No. 5** (the church office), pre-dates the building or re-building of **No. 6**. In the little courtyard at the side of **No. 6** look at the timber lintels over the window and door in the south-east wall. The style of moulding is *c.* 1600 and although they have almost certainly been re-set they are probably part of the earlier building on this site.

159 East gable of No.6 Church Street with blind windows.

187

160 Door with moulded lintel on No.6 Church Street.

161 Window with moulded lintel on No.6 Church Street.

162 Drawing showing Nos 8, 7, part of 5 at rear, and No. 6 Church Street.

163 Stone lintel within No. 8 Church Street.

Inspection of the rear range of **No. 7** has revealed a possible early eight-eenth-century roof with a two-storey seventeenth-century canted stone bay window on its south elevation. The 1840 map shows this building with a bay window on the north elevation adjacent to the street with its frontage in line with No. 8; it is likely that this bay was re-set on the rear.

Inside the mid to late eighteenth-century house **No. 8** (known as 'School House') there is a re-set stone lintel inscribed 'RISIT APOLLO' (Apollo smiles), probably a relic from the adjacent grammar school. Also found within the rear range of this property, when excavating the floor close to the party wall with the former school building, were the remains of a stone

189

164 Grammar school and schoolhouse (No. 8), *c.*1800.

newel stair. It is known that the cellars under the western end of the school (these were filled in when converted to a house in the 1960s) were accessed from No. 8, then used as the schoolmaster's house.

The **Vicarage** (which has no postal number) stands on the site of the original free grammar school that was founded by the Guild of the Holy Trinity in 1450 when it undertook to provide a fit person to instruct poor boys and scholars in grammar. Several buildings in Church Street belonged to medieval chantries; when these were dissolved in 1549 the houses passed to the Crown and were sold off to private purchasers. Some were bought at that time and others at a later date: in 1572 'a messuage on the south side of Church Street' and in 1590 'all that messuage and garden in Church Street which formerly belonged to the late dissolved Chantry of St. John Baptist'. The townsmen who purchased these buildings were acting as trustees so that the properties could be used by the grammar school and its schoolmaster. These houses were probably on the site of the present

165 Remodelled grammar school, c.1900.

166 Garden elevation of Redrobe House (No. 9 Church Street) early twentieth century.

vicarage which occupies a wide plot, and were later rebuilt as the school and adjoining schoolmaster's house. The varying ground-floor fenestration shown in Fig.164 seems to indicate more than one dwelling here with a later first-floor addition. The grammar school continued here until 1856 when its numbers declined and the building was in a state of disrepair. The former large vicarage stands on the opposite side of the road and was built in the 1860s as a replacement for an earlier building on that site.

Redrobe House, Nos 9 and 10 (formerly Yewdell & Eastville) was the town's workhouse from 1740 when it was built by Chipping Norton Corporation with the loan of a legacy of £100 from the will of the vicar Edward Redrobe. There may have been an earlier building on this site that was one of the former chantry properties in Church Street sold in 1549. The vestry minutes taken in May 1740 record that there were five trustees appointed to oversee the building of the workhouse and five members of the community were to act as managers. The person who became the first master of the workhouse was John Young and an inventory was taken in 1741 of all the contents of the building when he took on the post for a period of seven years. Eight rooms containing a total of fifteen beds were listed along with three other rooms, a hall and kitchen with cooking facilities and cellar. The next inventory taken seven years later in 1748, when George Slatter took over as master, contained ten rooms with twenty beds, two other rooms, hall, kitchen and cellar. The increased number of beds illustrates the need to accommodate more inhabitants. Look at the row of second-floor windows that can be seen from the street as you walk by; they have been painted on to the original recesses after they were blocked when more accommodation required the addition of new dormer windows at a higher level. This building became a private residence (**No. 9**) when the new Union workhouse was built in the London Road in 1835.

Continuing up the street you come to Whitehouse Lane, so-called because a Charles Whitehouse lived here in former times. If you refer to the 1840 map, you will notice that this access way suggests that it may have formed a 'back lane' behind the burgage plots on the lower side of the market place. If this is so, the lane would have exited into New Street at the point where the road widened (near the present Finsbury Place) and opposite the original manor house (see New Street section).

Cross the road and you will see the wonderful row of **almshouses** built in 1640 by Henry Cornish, one of the burgesses of the Corporation. He was a great benefactor of this town and, as he was not survived by any of his

167 Gateway to almshouses.

twelve children, left his money and property for the benefit of the poor of Chipping Norton. The gateway is contemporary with the almshouses and is constructed in ashlar stone with a cambered archway. Look up and you will see the motto inscribed there 'Remember the Poor'. These almshouses were originally built for 'eight poor widows to dwell in rent free' and to be the 'most aged, honest and of godly life and conversation'. Whilst standing at the gate, count the chimneys, nine in all; this is always a surprise as there were only eight cottages. Assumedly the blind chimney at the lower western end was added for the sake of symmetry. This building is constructed in coursed rubblestone with ashlar dressings and a stone-tiled roof. Each cottage has a two-light stone-mullioned window with a dripstone in the gable, and there are three-light windows on the ground floor under a continuous string course. In the 1950s, these cottages were refurbished and combined to make four larger houses available for widows of Chipping Norton, now at a subsidised rent. The plan in Fig.169 clearly shows the thick walls dividing the original eight dwellings, which were designed with one room on each floor and external privies in the rear yard area.

There is documentary evidence from *c*.1535 of an earlier almshouse in Chipping Norton although the site of this is unknown. It originally maintained 'six aged men', supported by the Guild of the Holy Trinity, but later must have included women. Some sixteenth-century wills included bequests such as '1 smock for 4 poor women in the alms house' and '12d in bread to 12 poor people in the almshouses'.

Back on the south side of the street you will notice a driveway leading to the **Old Manse**. This was rebuilt as a gentleman's residence in the early nineteenth century on to the end of the western range of **No. 8 Market Street**. Inspection of the eastern end revealed a truss in the present party wall which is visible in both properties. This clearly indicates that this range was formerly in one ownership, possibly a four-bay malthouse, and perhaps connected to the 'ancient messuage' that is known to have existed in Market Street.

Now continue towards the top end of Church Street and the property on the southern corner of its junction with Market Street. This house known as **No. 12 Market Street** has its rear wing running west down Church Street; this now-shortened range is shown on the 1840 map as a continuous building as far as the driveway to the Old Manse. An extract of a lease of 1718 mentions that this house was occupied by Jonathan Taylor (a son of William Taylor who lived in the Blue Boar). In 1720 Jonathan was fined

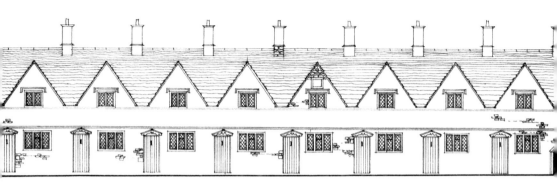

▲ 168 Drawing of south elevation of almshouses.

▼ 169 Ground-floor plan of almshouses: 1950s conversion to four units.

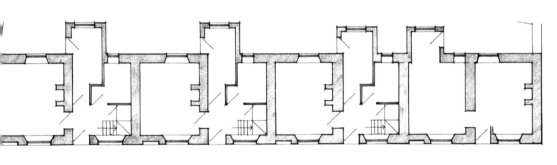

'2s.6d. for his stack of wood standing in the Church Street'; this seemed to be a common reason for many recorded fines. Later in 1832 part of this messuage, about seven bays, is described as 'standing at the north side of a former entry leading to an ancient messuage'. This implies that the entry must have led to the back of the properties in Market Street where we know that **Nos 7, 8 and 9** still have fifteenth- or sixteenth-century timbers within their structures.

The northern corner of Church Street, where it meets Spring Street, is proving to be a complex area. One of the interesting finds that has come to light is the site of a horsepond or pool which is shown on the 1840 map as No. 321. There is still a covered culvert in the courtyard behind **No. 5**

170 Twentieth-century view down Church Street.

171 No. 1 Church Street.

Spring Street indicating a connection to a water source. By 1894 the horsepool had gone and deeds mention 'a small piece of ground on the north side of Church Street whereon the town pump formerly stood'.

197

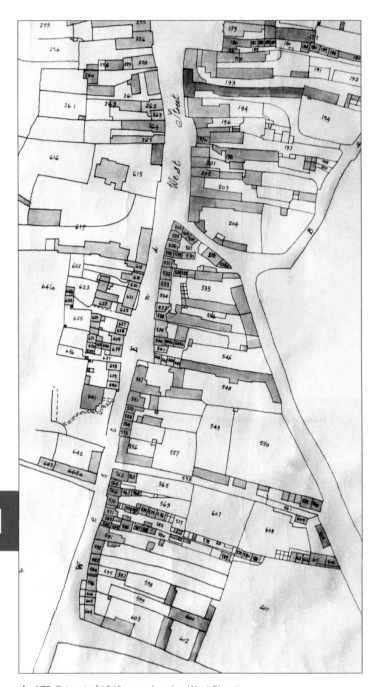

▲ 172 Extract of 1840 map showing West Street.

➤ 173 Walk map showing present numbering.

WEST STREET

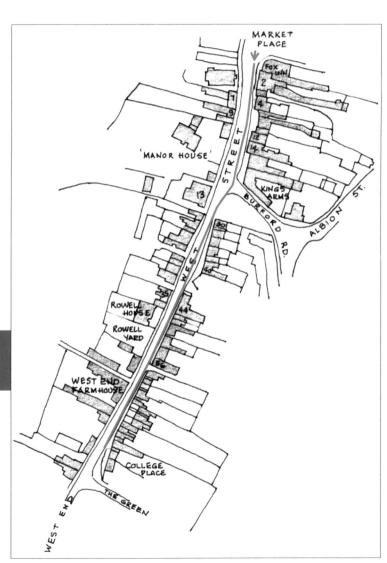

West Street

WALKING OUT of the south-west corner of Market Place you enter West Street, which is not due west as it implies. The name may have derived from the possibility of the road leading to the original west field in the open-field system which was in place before enclosure in 1770. Alternatively it may have been a minor road, west of the more important Woodstock to Burford road. There has always been confusion about the distinction between West End and West Street. Nowadays West Street begins at the Fox Hotel on the corner of Market Place and continues to The Green, where it becomes West End and eventually connects to the Churchill Road; before the nineteenth century this whole area was known as West End. Beyond the Burford Road corner it was mainly an agricultural suburb with several large farmhouses and a few small cottages. Closer to the market place the variety of buildings comprised small cottages and shops interspersed by grander houses, inns and the former parsonage house.

In the 1640s the large houses here included one called Cornishes on the site of the present Methodist church (**No. 5**). This was owned by Henry Cornish, the wealthy mercer who built the almshouses in Church Street. There were more shops here in later centuries, on both sides of the street, representing diverse trades. Note all the varying shop-window styles, some of which have now been incorporated into dwellings. There is a slight widening of the street just after it leaves the market place and the cellars beneath the buildings on the east side of this area also follow this line, indicating an earlier building-line. This wider area of the street may have been used for the sale of animals in the fairs of former times. Livestock were usually kept out of the main market area as denoted by the name 'Horsefair'

174 Drawing of west gable of the Fox and No. 2 West Street.

at the northern end of the town, although sheep were sold in High Street, indicated by the surviving sheepground leases of 1668.

Adjoining the Fox Hotel on the corner of West Street and Market Place is a large imposing six-bay building (**No. 2**) with an eighteenth-century facade and carriage archway. Note the date 1796 on the projecting keystone of the Gibbs-style pedimented doorway; this denotes the establishment of the brewery office and off-licence (called the **Rum Puncheon**) at these premises by James Hitchman. However, the facade you see today was added in the early eighteenth century. This property had been the Swan Inn from at least the beginning of the seventeenth century and was in the hands of the Hyatt family from the 1630s; by the 1650s it was held by the Jaquest family. Surviving inventories show how the inn expanded from Richard Jaquest's hostelry in 1668 to John Jaquest's more substantial business in 1713. The inventory at this time shows eleven chambers with twenty-four beds and a total value of £397 12s 10d. There were two cellars with beer and liquor worth £37. This vast stone-vaulted cellarage still survives and extends from West Street following the slope of Hitchman Mews. There is an exit at the eastern end of the present outbuildings which can be seen if you walk under the archway into the mews area. A curved recess in the rear stone wall of the present shop (Winebear) is evidence of a winder staircase rising from the cellars and possibly continuing up to the second floor.

▲ 175 Vaulted passageway between the cellars of Nos 2 and 4 West Street.

▼ 176 Barrel-vaulted cellar under No. 2 West Street.

177 Rear range of outbuildings behind No. 2 West Street.

On the opposite side of the street stands **No. 9**, another house with a handsome eighteenth-century ashlar frontage. This house together with the attached **No. 11** may have been one larger house, possibly symmetrical about a central carriage arch. Note the horizontal stone banding at first-floor level which continues across both buildings suggesting that it was of one build, but later divided into two dwellings. It is not known who actually built this house but in 1655, William Gardner, a collarmaker, lived on this site, in an earlier building. There have been many alterations to the present facade: look at the scars on the front elevation that indicate the position of former openings. The steeply pitched roof is set back behind an impressive, large, decorative overhanging bracketed cornice. There are three bays to No. 9, separated by two trusses at second-floor level of a similar type found elsewhere in town. These include an unusual type of interrupted tie-beam without a horizontal member; the chiselled carpenter's assembly marks are clearly shown on the timbers. In the eighteenth century the house belonged to Samuel West, a baker, with his bakehouse situated behind the premises. There is a fine early eighteenth-century staircase rising through the centre of the house and several internal features of the same period such as panelled doors, window shutters and fire-surrounds.

178 View through archway showing rear range of No. 2 West Street.

179 Drawing of Nos 9-11 West Street.

Back on the other side of the street are two houses, **Nos 12 and 14**, which, until recently, were used as a surgery. As you pass by, look at the cellar windows which are just visible at ground level; stone mullions and jambs with cavetto mouldings indicate the earlier origins of this building. The barrel-vaulted cellars hold the remains of stone winder stairs. The present facade was added *c.* 1730, probably built as one dwelling. The internal features in many of the rooms are consistent with the date of refronting, particularly in one of the first-floor rooms facing the street. An unusual feature found in this building was the use of red ochre pigment; this was seen on the walls of the cellars and also on external timber beams at the rear of **No. 12** where the corner of the wall is splayed to give enhanced access to the rear yard from the side passage.

180 Part of truss in No. 9.

181 Splayed corner with red ochre pigment at rear of No. 12 West Street.

182 Cellar under No. 12 West Street.

At the junction with Burford Road stands the King's Arms Hotel, **No. 18**, with another imposing eighteenth-century frontage concealing an earlier building. There are dressed stone quoins to the coursed and squared rub-blestone walls. Stand at the corner and note the splayed angle of the wall adjacent to Burford Road; look up at the chimney to see how the rear roof angle is adjusted to take account of this. Internally this corner consists of a substantial triangular block of stone with an inset lintel suggesting a former fireplace. Inside the bar seating area, at the rear, are three beams with cavetto mouldings which imply a possible sixteenth-century origin to this building which was a private house before becoming an inn in the nineteenth century. The cellars extend across the whole width of the property with three barrel-vaulted bays running parallel to the street. If you look along the pavement level you can see the remnants of the former stone-mullioned windows lighting the cellar areas; this is indicative of the building's earlier origins.

By far the largest property in this street is set back and hidden away behind trees and a stone wall. This has been called the **Manor House** since the 1890s (see New Street walk for information on the original manor house). It is an important building, possibly dating from the late fifteenth century, which belonged to Gloucester Abbey. It was originally known as the 'parsonage house', and was leased to a succession of tenants who farmed the abbey's land at Chipping Norton. The abbey was succeeded at the Reformation by the Dean and Chapter of Gloucester who owned this house until 1859. Formerly it stood in much larger grounds extending down into what is now New Street car park, and abutting the land belonging to the true manor house in New Street. The house is constructed of coursed rubble-stone with some stone dressings and quoins. The steeply pitched gable-end

183 Drawing of Nos 12-14 West Street.

184 Beam in rear of bar of the King's Arms, No. 18 West Street.

185 Second beam in rear bar area of the King's Arms.

of the original house can be clearly seen in the elevation that faces West Street (see Fig.188). Much alteration has been undertaken over the past 500 years but a fifteenth-century window does survive with some sixteenth-century features including stone-mullioned windows and lintels with cavetto mouldings. Many of the roof areas appear to have been raised, probably in the seventeenth century, thus making it difficult to predict what form the earlier house took.

Further down West Street on the eastern side is **No.44**, a building with a typical seventeenth-century gable, including three windows of diminishing sizes, facing northwards towards Market Place. Note the four large stone-mullioned windows on the street elevation. At the rear is a stair tower with an internal curved stone recess housing a winding staircase extending from cellar level to second floor. Although this type of tower is uncommon in Chipping Norton, a few examples have been found and they also occur in nearby villages. The main entrance to the house from the rear yard, opposite a large central chimney stack, suggests a lobby-entrance plan. Barrel-vaulted cellars also survive here with blocked splayed window reveals. The building was a farmhouse for many years, belonging to the wealthy yeomen farmers of the Guy family from the 1770s. This steeply pitched roof may have originally been covered with thatch, supported on the large timber trusses in which forelock bolts have been used where the collars have been raised to provide extra headroom on the second floor.

A property situated in the narrow part of this street, **No.56**, was the Bell Inn from the 1790s and incorporated the adjacent cottage of **No.54** at a later date. These properties were built as private houses, with No. 56 being of seventeenth-century date. They have now recently been converted back to two dwellings. The building has an interesting stone winder staircase down to the cellar and the remains of the curved recess in the stone wall continues up to the first floor. The position of the former entrance doorway is still evident in the wall adjoining the side lane, Bell Yard. The steeply pitched roof, now covered with stone slates, may have been thatched originally.

Set back behind a high stone wall in a narrower part of the street on the western side, stands the three-storey **Rowell's House** with its elegant ashlar facade incorporating a first-floor band and moulded cornice, see Fig.33. It was named for William Norman Rowell who lived there in the early twentieth century, an ironmonger who founded the Hub Ironworks in the town. Formerly in larger grounds incorporating the adjacent **Rowell's**

186 No.18 West Street (King's Arms).

187 Rear range of King's Arms along Burford Road.

188 Drawing of the 'Manor House', the former parsonage house.

Yard this was the site of a substantial farmhouse in the seventeenth century, owned by William Smythe. He left it to his daughter Anne Brayne from whom it descended in the Brayne family. By the 1650s and perhaps earlier, there was a tannery in the adjoining yard area. John Brayne, who died in 1744, was a wealthy tanner and he probably rebuilt the present house in the latest fashion. In 1760 it was described as 'very agreeable for a Gentleman and Family' and the house 'genteel and convenient, having a sashed Front next the Street, and a sashed Front towards the Fields, with a View for several miles'. Many surviving internal decorative features date from the eighteenth century and there is a large basement beneath the house, part of which is stone barrel-vaulted. A large five-light stone-mullioned window at the rear of the lower ground floor is a probable survival from the earlier farmhouse.

West End Farmhouse, **No.43**, stands adjacent to Stretchpool Lane, and is built of coursed rubblestone with dressed stone quoins and chamfered stone-mullioned windows. This six-bay house seems to originate from the seventeenth century and was part of a large farm with three yardlands (approx. 60 acres) occupied by the Trout family from the end of the sixteenth century. The farm was originally held by copyhold from the manor, and in 1683 Simon Trout purchased it from Edward Chadwell, whose great-grandfather had kept the land when he sold the manor in 1608. In

213

189 No. 44 West Street in 1957. (Photograph: P. Spokes)

190 Stair tower at rear of No. 44 West Street.

191 View of Bell Yard at side of No. 56 West Street.

addition to farming, the Trout family in the 1660s were tallow chandlers, rendering down animal fats to make candles. It later belonged to various farming families including Groves, Wheeler, Gibbs, Guy, Keck and Busby. The property has two stone barrel-vaulted cellars, similar to many others in the town, with former steps leading up to the rear yard. Just behind the northern end of the main range, now within the later western range, a deep circular well has been uncovered. Internally there are some surviving seventeenth-century features. The present front doorway may not have been the primary entrance as many farmhouses have their front face to the farmyard at the rear; there is evidence that this might be the case here. Note the small blocked window above the door from the street; this would have provided light to the winder staircase up to the attic. Alongside this window,

215

192 Basement window at rear of Rowell's House.

193 Cornice and panelled archway in Rowell's House.

194 West End Farmhouse (No. 43 West Street) and Stretchpool Lane.

under the eaves, is the Sun Fire Insurance plaque No. 320249 acquired by Groves Wheeler for £2 in December 1773 to insure the contents of his rickyard for £800.

Almost at the end of West Street is **College Place**, so called because it originally belonged to Brasenose College, Oxford. The property had been part of the estate of Cold Norton Priory and passed to the college after the priory was dissolved. An extensive collection of surviving leases in the college archives imply that the building was erected between 1609 and 1623 when it was in the possession of Robert Holder, a shoemaker, whose family had held the land since 1566. In 1636 the lease was assigned

195 Blocked windows in West End Farmhouse.

to John Norgrove, the vicar of Chipping Norton, who lived there until his death in 1659. His son Nehemiah and grandson John, both wealthy tanners who operated the tannery on the opposite side of the road, lived at College Place until 1719. When Nehemiah Norgrove died in 1693 his inventory recorded ten rooms in the house, with a cellar, garret and four outhouses. This property is now divided into two dwellings, **Nos 1 and 2 College Place**; compare Figs 199 and 200 and note the missing dormer windows.

196 Cellar under West End Farmhouse.

The original building appears to have been built as a cross-passage house. Note the labelled drip mouldings on the stone-mullioned windows and entrance doorway; the lintel over the door has been lifted at some former time to give extra height. A blocked cellar window is visible at pavement level which would have lit the small cellar chamber to **No. 1**, accessed by surviving winder steps from the ground floor. There is internal evidence of this winder stair formerly continuing up to the first floor to the north side of the large seventeenth-century stone fireplace. In a 1628 terrier (a description of lands and property) for Widow Holder, the tenement was described as 'consisting of a six-bay messuage, a large three-bay barn, a one-bay stable and a two-bay courthouse, with a backside and garden containing one quarter of an acre'; quite a substantial property.

219

▲ **197** Seventeenth-century entrance doorway to College Place, West Street.

➤ **198** Side jamb of fireplace in No. 1 College Place.

199 College Place *c.*1900 with dormer windows.

200 College Place, West Street in 2016.

∧ **201** Extract of 1840 map showing New Street.

➤ **202** Walk map showing present numbering.

NEW STREET

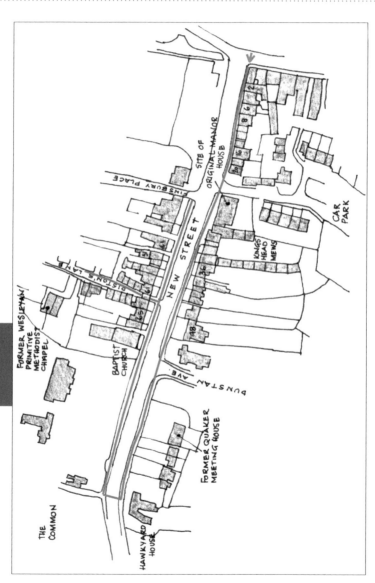

Walk 6

New Street

NEW STREET leads out of the market place in the south west corner; it is part of the main A44 that passes through the centre of town. Originally this was one of the narrow entrances into the market place but was widened in the 1960s. All the buildings that used to stand on the north side of the street were demolished from the top corner down to Finsbury Place, now replaced by a supermarket and car park. The origin of the name 'new' has always been a subject for much debate; it is generally accepted that it was probably the newest street to be added to the town shortly after the laying out of the market place in the twelfth century. The street led down to the great Common where there was a gate to stop the animals from straying into town. The route then continued on westwards in the direction of Worcester.

This walk begins on the southern side of the street by looking at the buildings which make up the corner property (**No. 10 Market Place and No. 2 New Street**) now estate agents and adjoining solicitor's offices. Note the straight joints between the two properties and the scars from former openings; all indications of radical alterations in former times. The positions of now-disused timber lintels at differing levels on the facade give clues to the changing floor levels that have occurred within the building. The present doorway to **No. 2** may well have been a passageway to the yard at the rear but now gives access to the stairway and a semi basement room. There is an unusual stair tower with a conical internal roof construction at the rear of these two properties tucked into the very constricted corner area behind them. This is a very confused jumble of buildings from various periods all vying for space and having to cope with the steep slopes presented by the topography.

203 View looking down New Street *c.*1800 showing house on site of original manor house and King's Head with archway.

As medieval remains have been found on the northern corner of New Street, it is more than likely that there would be remains of a similar period on the southern side; however, to date none have been found. The evidence for dating the row of buildings that stand here now all points towards the late seventeenth or early eighteenth century. The roof timbers that were recorded in **No. 2** and the winding stone stairs leading to the cellar of **No. 6** have all the hallmarks of this period. Indeed this is borne out by the date and initials that can be seen high up under the eaves of **No. 8** (see Fig.205).

In 1686 when Joseph Higgins, a bodicemaker, took over **No. 16**, he set about rebuilding an end wall on a narrow piece of land acquired from his neighbour, William Lord; there must have been an open area of land between **No. 16** and one of its neighbours at that time. A through-passage in the western half of this house suggests that it was formerly two separate properties, later converted to one dwelling; this has been found many times in Chipping Norton. There is also evidence in this building of the front roof pitch being raised from a lower eaves-line to provide more usable space on the second floor. It is likely that this was undertaken in the whole row around the time of that same date, due to the similarities in the street eleva-

225

◄ **204** No. 2 New Street.

▼ **205** Date and initials on No. 8 New Street.

206 Drawing of Nos 14-20 New Street.

JMA.Cliffe

tion. You will also notice that some houses in this row of buildings have rendered walls; probably due to the poor state of the stonework following much alteration. Unfortunately this obscures any features in the masonry which might otherwise provide clues to the former appearance. The rear range has a typical seventeenth-century steeply pitched gable with a central window to each storey in diminishing sizes. The interior also includes two large fireplace recesses, some timber studwork at intermediate level on an original rear wall and chamfered beams.

Walking further down the street on this southern side, you will notice the large building (now **Nos 28-32**) with a small cupola or bell tower on the ridge line. This is a remnant from its days as the British School, converted in 1854 from a former townhouse of *c.* 1730 date, but its history goes back much further; originally the site of the true manor house probably built in the fifteenth century when Richard Croft was lord of the manor of Chipping Norton (see Chapter 1).

It is speculated that the adjoining **King's Head Inn** may have been included in the complex of buildings belonging to the manor house. There is little documentary evidence for this three-storey seven-bay building but it is well worth noting the fine architectural features proudly displayed on its baroque eighteenth-century facade. This property is likely to have an earlier core, possibly built as a private house and later radically rebuilt as an inn with the addition of its ashlar frontage. It was an establishment of considerable size and it is surprising that little mention has come to light of its time as an inn. As you walk past the entrance to King's Head Mews, do look through and admire the area which was once the stable yard for this former coaching inn.

The documentary evidence shows that **Nos 34, 36 and 38** were all in the ownership of Michael Chadwell in the 1650s; he was the grandson of a former lord of the manor who had sold his lordship but retained most of his manorial property. By the 1680s Nos 36 and 38 had been sold and in the early eighteenth century they were divided into three dwellings. However, it appears that the radical alteration into the house we see today at **No. 36** was undertaken by Richard Fowler when he rebuilt the property as a single dwelling around 1790. The house has a handsome facade, although not completely symmetrical; this may reflect its former life as either two or three dwellings. The two ground-floor windows have finely moulded Tuscan-style columns set in tripartite sashes flanking an elegant doorway with a four-light rectangular fanlight, timber side pilasters and projecting hood supported on scrolled brackets. The cellar of this property has a three-light stone-mullioned window in the rear wall and much evidence of its former nineteenth-century use as a kitchen. It is also clear that this cellar connected to that under the adjacent No.38 with a red brick barrel-vaulted passage-way. The interior shows much evidence of former alterations, particularly in the reconfiguration of the staircase. However, there are still surviving internal features reflecting the grand 1790 townhouse. The adjoining house at **No. 38** shows clearly its former use as a coach house: see the stone vous-soirs outlining the former archway. When this property was sold in 1889, the details mentioned a harness room and stable. Note the wide doorway to the left of the arch which accesses a passage leading through to the rear outbuildings.

Walk on down the hill and cross over Dunstan Avenue and you will see, set back from the road, the former **Quaker meeting house**, now converted to two dwellings. The two large central arches were the original separate entrances for men and women; the only other openings were windows on the rear wall. The present building was erected in 1804 to hold some 200 people as a replacement for the original structure built in 1696 when there was a growing number of Quakers in the town.

207 South side of New Street with former King's Head and British School on site of original manor house, early twentieth century.

208 Drawing of Nos 34-38 New Street.

209 View looking east up New Street, *c.*1800.

Continue walking down New Street and you will notice a substantial house now called **Hawkyard House**, formerly Ivycroft. This house is positioned right on the edge of town where there was originally a gate leading on to the great Common. Formerly this house comprised two cottages facing New Street, possibly built in the late seventeenth or early eighteenth century. There is an existing cellar under the eastern end with the remains of a two-light stone-mullioned window on the rear south wall. The western wing which runs along the driveway facing the Common (see the corner of the building in Fig.209) may have been ancillary barns before being converted to extra residential use; there are surving lintels to suggest much larger openings. Evidence suggests that the rear north-south wing was originally separated from the main house by a through-passageway and later joined to the main accommodation. This is indicated by the awkward access openings from the first-floor landings with the change in floor levels.

On the northern side of New Street you will now walk past one of the areas of common land which still belong to the town. Continue up the hill until you come to the **Baptist church**. The building you can see from the road is the nineteenth-century enlargement in front of the original chapel which was built in 1733 by nonconformists. This still exists at the rear but has now been converted to residential use. The dissenters had previously met in members' houses with one of the notable early ministers being John

Thorley, a Presbyterian, who died in 1759. He had lived in a house behind
the Diston farmhouse mentioned next.

No. 65 and **No. 63** have been subdivided in different combinations over
the centuries. Look at the front elevation and see the stone plaque set in the
wall at the junction between the two present cottages inscribed 'Thomas
Frayne 1635'. By the time of his death in 1670, Thomas was an innkeeper in
High Street and his will bequeathed his house to his wife Mary and then to
his three daughters. This dwelling on the corner of New Street and Diston's
Lane was probably built as a farmhouse with all the barns and outbuildings
on land to the north. The present access to Diston's Lane, named after the
family who lived here from the end of the seventeenth century to the end
of the eighteenth century, formerly led through to the farmyard area. The
room over the lane was constructed during the nineteenth century, possibly
after No. 63 became separated from No. 65.

During the recording of this house it became clear that the western end
of No. 65, adjacent to No. 67, had been a separate one-bay building. There
were clear indications of the removal of a substantial stone wall to the right
of the present front entrance door, extending right through the whole height
of the building into the attics. The roof construction showed how the purlins

210 Drawing of Nos 63-67 New Street.

211 Thomas Frayne plaque on Nos 63-65 New Street.

212 Panelling in No. 65 New Street.

213 Chimney stack at rear of No. 65 New Street.

214 Fireplace in No. 63 New Street.

from one house had been connected to the purlins from the other house with extra timber and struts. This left a three-bay building (incorporating No. 63) to the east being the principal section, the Diston farmhouse. Also shown in the attic were the remains of a steeper pitched roof with a lower eaves level, beneath newer rafters, and evidence of a former thatched covering. Both present cottages contain large inglenook fireplaces and the one on the rear wall of No. 65 has a very large external chimney stack. There are examples of seventeenth- and eighteenth-century panelling in ground and first-floor rooms.

As you walk back up New Street towards the town centre, note the several gaps between the houses which lead down to other dwellings built on land at the rear; another common feature in Chipping Norton, where use has been made of every available space or outbuilding to accommodate more people.

Make your way back up the hill and admire the view of the west side of the splendid Town Hall, built in 1842, to a design by George Repton; this replaced the market house shown in Fig. 1.

215 Early twentieth-century view of narrow entrance to the market place at top of New Street.

216 Widened area at top of New Street in 2016.

GLOSSARY OF ARCHITECTURAL TERMS

abacus (pl. abaci)	slab forming top or capital of a column
Adam style	eighteenth-century neo-classical style from James and Robert Adam
architrave	moulded frame around a window or doorway
ashlar	smooth squared stone masonry laid in regular courses
assembly marks	used by carpenters to mark the timbers either side of a joint
backside	the area at side and rear of a dwelling
Baroque	architectural style from late seventeenth to mid-eighteenth centuries
barrel vault	continuous arched vault, semi-circular or segmental
bay	section between two roof trusses or truss and wall
blind window	blocked up window
bolection	heavy moulding used in late seventeenth- and eighteenth-century panelling
boss	projecting ornament concealing intersection of vaulting ribs
brackets	carved timber pieces to support a cornice or other feature

broach stop	splayed pointed angle at edge of masonry block
buttress	projection from a wall for additional support
cambered	with a slight curve, centre higher than the ends
cant	set at an angle
canted bay	bay window with angled sides
cantilever	part of a structure which is projected out over
cavetto	concave or hollow moulding
chamfer	an edge cut off at 45 degrees along length of beam or block
chancel	eastern part of church, housing main altar
charnel house	a place where bones are stored
corbel	projecting feature on a wall supporting another structure
cornice	moulded decorated projection at junction of wall and ceiling
coursed	masonry laid in regular horizontal courses
cranked principals	main rafters of truss with angle change giving a knee effect
cruck	primitive type of truss, usually curved, set up as an arch
crypt	underground cell or chapel
culvert	arched covering forming a passage for a water course
cupola	small dome on top of building
cyma	S-shaped moulding
dado	lower area of wall with a different treatment to upper part
dendrochronology	scientific method of dating timber
dentil	small rectangular block decoration on cornice

diminishing courses	roof slates laid in various sizes, smallest at ridge
Doric	one of the three orders of classical architecture
dripstone	projecting moulding on wall face above a door or window
eared architrave	lateral extension in corner of architrave of window or door
eaves	projection of roof over wall
encroachment	part of a building that extends over its original boundary
entry	the entrance or passageway to a dwelling
facade	main elevation of a building
fanlight	glazed section above a doorway
fenestration	window style and arrangement
forelock bolts	triangular wedges with bolt to clamp timbers together
frieze	horizontal decorated panel at eaves level
gargoyle	projecting, grotesquely carved water spout
garret	attic room
Gibbs style	in the Baroque style of architect James Gibbs (1682-1754)
H & L hinges	door hinges used in the seventeenth/eighteenth century
hall house	main living area of dwelling open to roof level
hood, drip mould	projecting moulding on wall face above a door or window
hopperhead	lead receptacle at eaves to collect roof rainwater
Ionic	one of the three orders of classical architecture
jamb	side of a window or doorway
jettied floor	a first floor projecting over a ground floor wall

238

jowl post	timber post with flares at top and/or bottom to give support
keystone	central stone in an arch which keys whole structure together
label	the turned-down corners of a hood mould
messuage	dwelling with adjoining lands in one ownership
metopes	plain recessed spaces between triglyphs in a Doric frieze
mortice	cavity cut into timber beam to receive a tenon
mullion	vertical bar dividing the lights of a window
neo-Georgian	late nineteenth-century revival of Georgian architecture
neo-gothic	nineteenth-century style simulating medieval gothic
newel	post around which stairs wind
niche	recessed area in a wall
ochre	colour made from fine clay; red, brown, yellow earthy colours
ogee	an S-shaped moulding
oolitic limestone	from the Jurassic period extending over the Cotswold Hills
ovolo	seventeenth-century moulding which curves outwards from its face
Palladian window	large three-section window with centre part arched
parapet	vertical extension of a wall hiding an internal gutter
pediment	triangular gable over a classical portico or doorway
peg	wooden dowel to hold timbers together at joint
pilaster	ornamental column on wall face with a slight projection
postholes	cut feature where a former post stood

principal rafter	top members of a truss
purlins	horizontal timbers to support rafters in roof construction
quadripartite	divided into four sections
quatrefoil	decorative shape of four partially overlapping circles
quoins	dressed corner stones of a building
raised cruck	truss with curved blades and collar, feet sitting on outer wall
render	plastered surface to timber framed wall
ribs	stone partition elements in vaulting
ridge piece	timber at highest point of roof structure
rubblestone	rough walling of unsquared stone
rustication	masonry blocks with rough surface and wide joints
scars	visible signs of alteration in building fabric
scroll stops	ogee-shaped stop to chamfer end on timber beam
sherd	fragment of pottery
sill beam	beam at base of timber framed wall
spandrel	the corner space between an arch and its enclosure
spine beam	internal beam parallel to ridgeline
springer	the point at which a vault rises from a vertical shaft
string course	horizontal band of masonry, slightly projecting
stucco	plaster of lime and fine sand used for decorative features
tenement	dwelling and all its outbuildings, gardens etc.
tenon	projection at end of a timber which sits into a mortice hole
tie beam	bottom member of a roof truss spanning between walls

tracery	stonework elements to support glass in a window
transverse beam	internal beam at right angles to ridgeline
trestle-sawn	timbers pre-1540
triglyph	vertical ribbed tablets with plain recessed spaces between
tripartite	divided into three parts
truss	timber construction to create a substantial support for roof
Tuscan columns	simplified Doric order
undercroft	underground chamber with vaulted ceiling
voussoirs	shaped masonry blocks within an arch
wallplate	beam running along top of wall at junction with roof timbers
wind braces	diagonal timbers to tie rafters together to prevent movement
winder	tread of a circular staircase

FURTHER READING
AND SOURCES

Arkell, T., Evans, N. and Goose, N., *When Death Do Us Part: Understanding and Interpreting the Probate Records of Early Modern England* (Leopard's Head Press: 2000)

Aston, M. and Bond, J., *The Landscape of Towns* (Sutton: 1987)

Brooks, A. and Sherwood, J., *Oxfordshire North and West* (Pevsner Architectural Guides: Buildings of England) (Yale University Press: 2017)

Brunskill, R.W., *Vernacular Architecture: An Illustrated Handbook* (Faber: 4th edn 2000)

Catchpole, A., Clark, D. and Peberdy, R., *Burford: Buildings and People in a Cotswold Town* (Phillimore: 2008)

Chambers, R.A., 'Excavations at No. 12 Market Place, Chipping Norton, Oxon.', *Oxoniensia*, 40 (1975), pp. 211-18

Chipping Norton Conservation Area Character Appraisal, 2013 (West Oxfordshire District Council)

Cliffe, J., *Chipping Norton High Street* (Chipping Norton Museum: 2014)

Clifton-Taylor, A., *The Pattern of English Building* (Faber & Faber: 1987)

Dyer, C., *A Country Merchant, 1495-1520: Trading and Farming at the End of the Middle Ages* (Oxford University Press: 2012)

Cunnington, P., *How Old is Your House?* (Marston House: 1999)

Eddershaw, D., *Chipping Norton: The Story of a Market Town* (Poundstone Press: Chipping Norton: 2006)

Hall, L., *Period House Fixtures and Fittings 1300-1900* (Countryside Books: 2005)

Hindle, B.P., *Medieval Town Plans* (Shire: 1990)

Lewis, D., *Chipping Norton Inns* (Chipping Norton Museum: 2004)

Morris, R., *Churches in the Landscape* (Dent: 1989)

Platt, C., *The English Medieval Town* (Secker & Warburg: 1976)

Rodwell, K.A. (ed.), *Historic Towns in Oxfordshire: A Survey of the New County* (Oxfordshire Archaeological Unit: Oxford: 1975)

Simons, E., Phimester, J., Webley, L. and Smith, A., 'A Late Medieval Inn at the White Hart Hotel, Chipping Norton, Oxfordshire', *Oxoniensia*, 70 (2005), pp. 309-23

Tiller, K. and Darkes, G. (eds.), *An Historical Atlas of Oxfordshire* (Oxfordshire Record Society 67, 2010)

Victoria County History of Oxfordshire, vols 10 (Banbury), 12 (Woodstock), 14 (Witney): all are available at British History Online (www.british-history.ac.uk).

SOURCES FOR THE HISTORY OF CHIPPING NORTON'S EARLY BUILDINGS

The main source of information on the ownership and occupiers of a building will often be the *summary of deeds* for the property at Chipping Norton Museum (see the museum's website at www.chippingnortonmuseum.org.uk for opening hours and contact details). In most cases the deeds themselves do not survive but a summary will contain information about changes in ownership, mortgages and use of the building.

Another informative source may be the *wills and inventories* compiled for probate after a death. Property owned by the deceased may be bequeathed in the will, and the probate inventory will list the possessions of the deceased and may name the rooms in a house. All the surviving probate documents for Chipping Norton before 1750 have been transcribed by the Chipping Norton Historical Research Group, and the transcripts are available on CD at the Chipping Norton Museum. The transcripts can also be seen at the Oxfordshire History Centre in Oxford (www.oxfordshire.gov.uk/cms/public-site/oxfordshire-history-centre) which holds most of the originals. Some wills and a few inventories are held at The National Archives at Kew in London (www.nationalarchives.gov.uk/help-with-your-research/research-guides/wills-1384-1858/).

From 1753 Oxfordshire had a local newspaper, *Jackson's Oxford Journal*, in which advertisements and reports often included valuable information about property. Editions of the newspaper from 1753-1900 can be searched online at the Oxfordshire History Centre and at the larger public libraries in Oxfordshire.

The *Map of Chipping Norton in 1840* illustrating the chapter on each street was drawn up to show properties liable for the poor rate and other local taxes collected by the parish vestry. The original map is in the Chipping Norton Museum. The copy reproduced in this book was drawn by Janice Cliffe.

Photographers were working at Chipping Norton by the 1870s and there are useful collections of *early twentieth-century photographs* which may show buildings before restoration or demolition. The photographs of Frank Packer, who had a photography business in the town from about 1907, are especially well known. Many photographs have been put online at www.pictureoxon.com by the Oxfordshire Museums Service. The Chipping Norton Museum also has an extensive collection of photographs, which can be seen at the museum: for contact details see www.chippingnortonmuseum.org.uk.

Finally, the plan and fabric of *the building itself* may provide clues to its original form and later development. A detailed report on each of the buildings surveyed by the Chipping Norton Buildings Record has been compiled with a full description, photographs, and in some cases plans, as well as any probate inventories, and summaries of deeds from the Chipping Norton Museum. These reports will be deposited at the Oxfordshire History Centre in Oxford.

Most buildings constructed before 1750 will be on the National Heritage List for England and a brief description of each Listed building can be found at https://www.historicengland.org.uk/listing/the-list/.

See also these websites:

- Oxfordshire Buildings Record, with links to further resources: www.obr.org.uk
- Historic England: https://historicengland.org.uk
- House history sources in Oxfordshire: www.oxfordshire.gov.uk/cms/content/house-history

PICTURE CREDITS

The authors are grateful to the following for permission to reproduce their material. References are to Fig. numbers.

Chipping Norton Buildings Record: 9, 10, 11, 12, 13, 14, 15, 16, 17, 18, 19, 20, 21, 22, 25, 26, 27, 29, 31, 33, 36, 37, 38, 40, 42, 48, 49, 50, 51, 52, 53, 55, 56, 58, 59, 60, 61, 62, 63, 64, 65, 69, 71, 72, 73, 74, 75, 76, 80, 82, 87, 93, 94, 95, 99, 100, 101, 102, 106, 107, 111, 112, 113, 114, 117, 123, 124, 125, 126, 127, 128, 129, 131, 135, 136, 137, 138, 141, 142, 143, 144, 145, 146, 147, 148, 151, 152, 153, 154, 155, 156, 157, 159, 160, 161, 163, 167, 171, 175, 176, 177, 178, 180, 181, 182, 184, 185, 186, 187, 190, 191, 192, 193, 194, 195, 196, 197, 198, 200, 204, 205, 211, 212, 213, 214, 216

Chipping Norton Museum: 30, 32, 34, 45, 46, 54, 68, 81, 83, 89, 92, 96, 118, 119, 120, 139, 149, 164, 165, 166, 170, 199, 203, 207, 209, 215

Chipping Norton Town Council: 1

Janice Cliffe: 2, 3, 5, 6, 43, 44, 47, 53, 57, 66, 67, 70, 77, 78, 79, 84, 85, 86, 88, 91, 97, 98, 103, 104, 105, 108, 109, 115, 116, 121, 122, 130, 132, 133, 134, 140, 150, 158, 162, 168, 169, 172, 173, 174, 179, 183, 188, 201, 202, 206, 208, 210

Historic England: (Britain from Above) 4, 7; (P.S. Spokes) 28, 39, 41, 90, 110, 189

Oxfordshire History Centre: 23, 24, 35

INDEX

Streets, buildings and subjects relate to Chipping Norton except where stated. Place-names are in Oxfordshire if not shown otherwise. Italics refer to Figure numbers of illustrations.

Emmelina, 15
Enslow Bridge, 46
Enstone, 26, 73
Eton College chapel, 28
Evesham (Worcs), 15, 56

fairs, 23, 67, 125, 200
farmhouses, 41, 57, 59, 61, 64, 69-70,
    72, 81, 174, 200, 211, 213, 215, 231-4
farming, 15, 24, 41, 49, 54, 57-9, 62, 64,
    67-70, 118, 200, 213, 215
Fawler family, mercers and woollendrap-
    ers, 128, 130; *34*
Faytour, Richard le, woolman, 26
fire insurance, 165, 217
fireplaces and fire-surrounds, 59-62, 79,
    99, 133, 148, 161, 165, 174, 203, 208,
    219, 227, 234; *30, 126, 131-2, 144-5,
    198, 214*
Fitzalan family, 15, 17-19, 23, 26, 32, 37;
    and see Arundel, earls of
Fowler, Richard, 228
Fox Hotel (2 Market Place), 25, 62, 75,
    144-8, 200; *8, 105, 174*
Frayne, Thomas, innkeeper, 108, 231;
    211
Fryday, Thomas, mason, 37, 180

gaol, 37, 128, 130-1
Gardner, William, collarmaker, 203
geology, 18; *5*
George Inn, medieval, 39, 48; (4 New
    Street), 75
Gerveys: Margaret, 28; Thomas, wool-
    man, 27
glaziers, 51, 62, 76-7, 172
Gloucester: Abbey, 15, 41, 209; Dean
    and Chapter, 15, 209
glovers, 51, 69-70, 168
Glyme Farm, 12
Glympton, 73-4; *3*

Goddard's Lane, 24, 51, 70; *2, 77-8*
Goddard's Lane buildings, 120-5; *81-5*;
    and see Blue Anchor; Blue Boar;
    Chequers
Goodwine, John, currier, 132
grammar school, 34, 40, 45-6, 48, 73,
    189-92; *163-5*
Great Tew, 56
Green, The, 19, 200; *2*
grocers, 27, 53, 72, 91, 172
guild of the Holy Trinity, 34, 36, 40,
    45-6, 48-9, 137, 190, 194; *17*
Guildhall, 36, 41, 45-6, 48, 51, 73, 135-
    40, 186; *18, 96-101*
Guildhall Yard, 24, 121-2
Guy family, 127, 211, 215

haberdashers, 53, 73
Hanwell, 37, 48
Harneplace (1 Market Place), 25; *8*
Harris: John, physician, 172; Samuel,
    haberdasher, 53
Hastings: George, 120; William, town
    clerk, 173
Hawkins, Robert, carpenter, 79
Hawkyard House (New Street), 230
Hayes, William, slatter, 60
hearth tax (1662), 57, 64, 67, 90, 99,
    144, 146
Henshaw: James, maltster, 60-1; family,
    52
Hesdin, Ernulf de, 12, 15-16
Heythrop, 32, 48, 73; *3*
Heythrop House, 81
Higgins: Joseph, bodicemaker, 225;
    Samuel, 77
high cross, 37
High Street (Upper Row, Top Row,
    Topside), 18-19, 22-4, 36-7, 51, 68,
    75, 89-115, 118, 156, 201; *2, 7, 32,
    43-4*

Stokes, John, mercer, 27

stone, as building material, 37, 41-2, 76, 80

stone slates, 37, 77, 114, 194, 211; *20*

stonemasons, 51, 62, 76, 81-2, 84, 94, 135

stone-quarries, 18, 37, 76, 81, 94

Stow-on-the-Wold (Glos), 15, 19, 41, 55, 56; *3*

Stratford, Robert, 39

Stratford-upon-Avon (Warws), 19, 36, 56

Stretchpool Lane, 213

Strong, Edward and Thomas, masons, 83, 94

subdivision of buildings, 62, 64, 76, 79, 82, 133, 168, 173, 176, 203, 228; *42*

Sussex, 26

Swan Inn (2 West Street), 51, 56-7, 74, 82, 148, 201; *174-8*

tailors, 51, 62, 73, 159

Talbot Inn (3-4 High Street), 11, 56-7, 74, 82, 93; *1, 35*

tallow-chandlers, 27, 51, 69, 127

Tanner: John le, 24; Thomas, mercer, 172

tanneries, 40, 52, 70, 72, 122, 168, 176, 213, 218

tanners, 27, 52, 69-70, 176, 213

Tarless, John, 176

taverns, 39, 100, 105

Taylor: Thomas, mason, 76; family, ropemakers, 75, 82, 121, 194

Taynton, Richard de, 24

Taynton, quarries, 94

Teiha daughter of Luke, 177

Thames, river, 15, 69

thatch, 17, 37, 57, 76-7, 211, 234

Thomas: Walter, town clerk, 61, 144; William, town clerk, 69, 144, 146

Thorley, John, Presbyterian minister, 230-1

Tidmarsh, Giles, shoemaker, 132

timber-framing, 37, 39, 78, 94, 101, 131-4, 159, 165, 171, 173-4, 227; *137-8*

tinsmiths, 73

Toft, Anthony and William, 144

Town Hall (1842), 11, 51, 137, 144, 148, 153, 234; *22, 46*

Trotyn, William, 24

Trout: Simon, 68; family, tallow-chandlers, 213, 215

Turner, Thomas, tailor, 62

turnpikes, 74

undercroft (20 High Street), 39, 41, 104-6, 241; *61-7*

Unicorn Inn (14 Market Place), 75, 149-50; *110*

upholsterers, 73, 79

vicarage houses, 46, 190, 192

vicars, 25, 41, 46, 52, 73, 192

Victoria Place, 158

Wales, 56, 79

wall-painting, 56, 99

Walter, Thomas, husbandman, 60

Ward: Hannah, 82; John, 119, 176

Warde, William, maltster, 160, 165

Waring family, blacksmiths, 134, 138

Waring's Lane, 134, 138

water supply, 12, 18, 23, 40, 51-2, 64, 79, 121, 124, 138, 141, 168, 176, 196-7, 215

Watery Lane, 40

weavers, 27, 51, 70, 72

wells, *see* water supply

Welsh Marches, 15, 26, 32

West, Samuel, baker, 81, 203

West End Farmhouse (43 West Street), 51, 59, 68, 213, 215, 217; *27, 194-6*

The destination for history